THE TRANSFORMATION OF INITIAL TEACHER EDUCATION

Tracing the development of initial teacher education since the large-scale expansion of the teaching profession after the Second World War to the present day, *The Transformation of Initial Teacher Education* explores the changing nature of teacher training.

Examining the growth of the 'teaching industry', this book addresses key issues including:

- the return to an apprentice model;
- the growing importance of schools in initial teacher education;
- the continuing decline in the role played by higher education;
- an examination of the broader socio-economic context of increased marketisation;
- a reconsideration of the international political factors driving the reform process; and
- interviews with prominent individuals who have been involved with the development of policy.

Considering the ideas and ideals that have permeated teacher education and how these have shaped the experiences of trainees on a variety of programmes across a broader international context, this book examines the future of teacher education and the changing nature of teaching, providing essential insight for trainee teachers, school staff and any academics involved in teacher education.

Ian Abbott is an Associate Professor in the Centre for Education Studies at the University of Warwick. He was previously the Director of the Centre and prior to that led the University's Institute of Education. He has worked with in partnership with a number of external organisations, including Teach First and Teaching Leaders. He has collaborated with a number of schools and colleges on a range of research and staff development projects. He has extensive experience of initial teacher education and has worked on a range of programmes. He has written extensively on a range of education policy issues including a number of books on aspects of secondary teacher education.

Mike Rathbone was Director of Continuing Professional Development in the Institute of Education at the University of Warwick. He has wide-ranging experience of primary teacher training and has worked in a number of schools and higher education institutions. He has published widely on teacher education and continuing professional development, especially related to beginning teachers.

Philip Whitehead began his career in education teaching in a comprehensive school in London in 1972. Since then he has worked across most phases of education including secondary, further, higher and special education. He was the headteacher of a secondary school in Papua New Guinea for three years. On returning to the UK he took management roles in staff development and teacher training, before moving into development work in higher education. He has carried out research into learning journeys and ethnicity, leadership cultures, educational policy, and professional development. At present he is Assistant Professor in Educational Leadership and Management at the University of Nottingham.

THE TRANSFORMATION OF INITIAL TEACHER EDUCATION

The Changing Nature of Teacher Training

Ian Abbott, Mike Rathbone and Philip Whitehead

Routledge
Taylor & Francis Group

LONDON AND NEW YORK

First published 2019
by Routledge
2 Park Square, Milton Park, Abingdon, Oxon OX14 4RN

and by Routledge
52 Vanderbilt Avenue, New York, NY 10017

Routledge is an imprint of the Taylor & Francis Group, an informa business

© 2019 Ian Abbott, Mike Rathbone and Philip Whitehead

The right of Ian Abbott, Mike Rathbone and Philip Whitehead to be identified as authors of this work has been asserted by him/her/them in accordance with sections 77 and 78 of the Copyright, Designs and Patents Act 1988.

All rights reserved. No part of this book may be reprinted or reproduced or utilised in any form or by any electronic, mechanical, or other means, now known or hereafter invented, including photocopying and recording, or in any information storage or retrieval system, without permission in writing from the publishers.

Trademark notice: Product or corporate names may be trademarks or registered trademarks, and are used only for identification and explanation without intent to infringe.

British Library Cataloguing in Publication Data
A catalogue record for this book is available from the British Library

Library of Congress Cataloging-in-Publication Data
A catalog record has been requested for this book

ISBN: 978-0-415-73873-6 (hbk)
ISBN: 978-0-415-73874-3 (pbk)
ISBN: 978-0-429-42456-4 (ebk)

Typeset in Bembo
by Taylor & Francis Books

CONTENTS

List of illustrations	*vi*
Preface	*vii*

1	Introduction	1
2	The early days of teacher training	10
3	The consensus in education begins to unravel	25
4	Teacher education as a competitive market	46
5	Current government policy	64
6	International perspectives	75
7	Models of provision: higher education	92
8	Models of provision: school-based	108
9	Teach First	120
10	Conclusion	131

References	*143*
Index	*153*

ILLUSTRATIONS

Figures

7.1 Comparison of PTES results	102
7.2 Providers with the highest and lowest employment rates	102
7.3 2017 Postgraduate Taught Experience Survey results	103
7.4 2017 Postgraduate Taught Experience Survey results	103

Table

7.1 PGCE applications and student numbers	100

PREFACE

This book considers the policy and practice of initial teacher education (ITE) in England by tracing the history and development of ITE from the earliest beginnings. It continues by looking at the implications of that development on policy and practice in the modern era. These changes are subsequently set in a broader international context.

The historical background deals briefly with the period in England before the Second World War and continues with a more detailed analysis of events since the war. The implications of significant reports into aspects of education in general and teacher education in particular are traced as is the process by which teacher training policy moved from being a preserve of 'experts' in education to an ideological tool of government.

Issues such as a return to the apprenticeship model, the increase in school involvement and the decline of the role of higher education in teacher training are put under the microscope. Inevitably, aspects of teacher recruitment and the changing nature of teaching are considered.

The book uses a series of interviews with individuals who have been involved in the development of policy including headteachers, directors of training organisations, higher education providers and officials of the Training Agency, but also with teachers who have acted as mentors in schools, newly qualified teachers and prospective teachers who are presently in training

An analysis of the issues raised is set alongside issues derived from research in the field and considered against the background of present developments in England. As attainment in education has been increasingly assumed to coincide with the economic prosperity of a nation comparisons of attainment in England with that of other nations has become common, using for example the Organisation for Economic Co-operation and Development Programme for Student Assessment. These sometimes unflattering comparisons have led to comparisons with teacher training practices in other 'competitor' countries such as the United States, Singapore and China.

Even though, as Professor Harvey Goldstein (*Guardian*, Letters, 7 December 2016) has pointed out, such comparisons need to be treated with care, in recent years secretaries of state for education in England have stressed the importance of international comparisons. In this book we examine teacher training practices in other parts of the world and utilise our experience of working with students and serving teachers in Africa, Asia, North America, the Arabian Gulf and various European countries.

Few people close to education doubt that teacher training in England is in turmoil. Changes and development are announced frequently, as for example the teaching apprenticeships announced by the Department for Education in October 2017 and the earlier white paper 'Education Excellence Everywhere' (2016, www.gov.uk), in which the then education secretary, Nicky Morgan, announced that the government would strengthen university- and school-led training by increasing the rigour of ITT content, putting a greater focus on subject knowledge and evidence-led practice whilst continuing to move to a school-led system. New criteria would be used for ITT providers with qualified teacher status being superseded by a system based on greater classroom effectiveness. In addition, similar changes were to be introduced in the strengthening of professional development provision for serving teachers.

Teacher recruitment has gone from bad to worse, as exemplified by the debacle of the National Teaching Service initiative to put 'elite' teachers into struggling schools. Launched in 2015 and discontinued a year later, the scheme, which reputably cost over £200,000, recruited only 24 teachers in spite of promising teachers £10,000 relocation expenses. The Public Accounts Committee reached the following conclusion in their report of June 2016: 'Ministers have "no plan" to meet the growing teacher shortage in England – teacher training targets have been missed for four successive years' (2016). Secretaries of state for education continue to face the same issue with evidence set out in July 2017 that a quarter of teachers who qualified in 2011 had left the profession within four years (Education Policy Unit).

The chair of the Public Accounts Committee Meg Hiller said that the government had taken too little responsibility for getting recruitment right and that the Department for Education remained woefully aloof from concerns raised by staff in schools and the freely available evidence. All of which, she concluded, puts at risk the educational attainment of pupils and consequently their life chances.

The 2016/17 reports came out as almost all political interest was centred on the European Union referendum and thereafter on the implications of the result. As a consequence, education secretaries were changed quickly depending on their view of the referendum and reports on education were largely ignored by the press and apparently also by politicians. It is possible to argue that this disturbing state of affairs is one result of education policy becoming a 'political football', a process which has been going on since 1976 when the then prime minister Jim Callaghan's speech at Ruskin College expressed concern about standards in educational attainment. He required his education secretary Shirley Williams to make changes in order to improve attainment, thus initiating the involvement of politicians in micro-managing education practice which is now commonplace (Abbott et al., 2013).

The changes in education policy as a whole which started almost 50 years ago have increased in momentum and scope to include the recruitment of school governors, the forced academisation of schools and the increasing influence of commercial and religious organisations on schools and schoolchildren. Teacher training has not been exempt from this continual upheaval and these policy developments have had a significant impact on the schools, children, their teachers and headteachers. Future teachers run the risk of not being equipped to think for themselves with policy makers assuming that there is a right and a wrong way to teach, forgetting the immense diversity of schools, children and practitioners (Alexander et al., 2010).

The authors of this book have worked in education in the United Kingdom and elsewhere for over 40 years – both as tutors in institutions concerned with teacher education and prior to that as schoolteachers. Their experience ranges from teaching in nursery, primary and secondary schools (frequently with students in training) to working as tutors, heads of department and directors of programmes, etc. in teacher training colleges, polytechnics, colleges of higher education and universities across the United Kingdom and abroad. They have taught with two-year-trained ex-service personnel, worked within school/college partnerships, the Graduate Teacher Scheme, School-Centred Initial Teacher Training, Teach First, School Direct and other programmes of training. They have all been instrumental in putting government initiatives into practice and working with schools and other providers and continue to do so.

In addition, their own very varied training as teachers has enabled them to consider how it has helped, or perhaps hindered, their own teaching practices and brings to bear a practical knowledge of the positive and negative aspects of various forms of teacher training – valuable at a time when many far-reaching changes are taking place in teacher training.

We would argue that teacher training has to include sections that are carried out as practice in schools and which will become meaningful only if they are preceded and followed by careful consideration of how various practices will most benefit the children and trainee. The latter need to consider what to look for in a school, the teachers and the children. Afterwards, there must be an opportunity for reflection with others about the practice and on how to apply lessons learned to subsequent experience.

We would argue that whereas there had been an over-reliance on a theoretical approach to the training of teachers, this has steadily and sensibly shifted towards an emphasis on the work in schools. However, by 2016 it has been allowed to move almost entirely to a 'teaching as a craft' approach where any theoretical content is ignored. Largely, too, this movement has not been backed by a 'research into policy' approach, although the words 'evidence based' frequently appear in policy statements (see for example DfE, 2015 and 2016a).

As will be seen in the book this and other questions were in the minds of the early pioneers in teacher training as they argued about the proportions of practical teaching practice and theoretical considerations needed to train effective teachers.

The contributions in the book detailing present practice in ITE are concerned with the experiences of those at the 'chalk face' and aims to give a flavour of the reality of the range of training routes now being offered. The book concludes with some speculation about likely future developments in teacher training.

This book will be of value to those engaged in ITE in England and elsewhere in the world and in addition to those studying on undergraduate and postgraduate education programmes. In particular, it is expected that those teaching staff and trainees in schools who have only recently become involved in ITE will find it of direct relevance to their work.

We owe a huge debt of gratitude to all the staff and students involved in ITE and professional development who contributed their experience to this book, especially Laura Abbott, Jennifer Barker, Jenny Bosworth, Karen Crawley, Kate Mawson, Laura Meyrick, Lauren Mintey, Reuben Moore, Jennifer Parker and Rebecca Reeve. We are extremely grateful to Rebecca Rooum for her invaluable help in finalising the manuscript.

We need to thank staff within the University of Warwick Institute of Education, the University of Worcester Institute of Education and the University of Gloucester School of Education for access to historical data.

1

INTRODUCTION

The importance of high-quality teaching in ensuring an outstanding education system has long been recognised. As a consequence, there has been increased interest in many countries in the way in which teachers are trained and are able to access professional development throughout their career. There can be little doubt that the overall quality of the teaching profession and the lessons they provide to their students will have a significant impact on the education system as a whole. High-quality teaching will lead to rising educational standards and an overall improvement in the system. Therefore, it is essential to ensure that the correct building blocks are in place to attract sufficient numbers and high-quality candidates, and to provide them with high-quality teacher training that will prepare them for future careers in the classroom. Hopefully, effective training will also contribute to improved teacher retention and reduce the number of teachers who leave the profession within a few years of qualification.

This chapter will consider the nature of teacher education and the debate between theory and practice, which has been at the root of many of the policy initiatives that have been introduced in recent years. In particular, it will consider the importance of teacher education in reforming education systems and potentially improving pupil outcomes. The significance of political interventions will also be discussed and the ongoing changes in the relationship between higher education (HE) and schools will be considered.

The growth of neoliberalism

Abbott, Rathbone and Whitehead (2013: 132) have outlined the importance of 'the new and modernisation' that has been at the centre of public-sector reform in the United Kingdom (UK) and in many other parts of the world. In the 1980s, partly in response to the economic problems many countries had experienced in the 1970s, neoliberal policies were widely introduced. In England this involved the breaking down of the post-war consensus and the development of a market-led system. Education along with other parts of the public sector became subject to the demands of the market, which should be influenced by 'the logic of the market place' (Ball, 2003a: 8). It is worth recording that the drive to a market-led system or marketisation was less apparent in other parts of the UK, especially Scotland, as education policy was largely left to the devolved governments to administer.

An ongoing series of policy reforms in England have had a profound impact on the education system. Schools have been given greater autonomy, with new types of school being established, for example academies and free schools. The importance of the local authority has been diminished and schools have been encouraged to compete for pupils and resources. As a consequence of these pressures, new entrants have been encouraged to enter the education market to provide a range of services. In England, new schools have been opened in an attempt to stimulate competition and increase choice. Most significant are the growth of academy schools, often operating as a multi-academy trust (MAT). Academy schools have been given greater freedom and, although funded by the state, are free from local authority or district control. A MAT is comprised of 'a number of individual schools, but there is one organisation that actually runs the schools' (Middlewood et al., 2018: 10). Given the growth of these new types of organisation, freed from traditional controls, it is a logical step for them to take a greater role in the initial training and professional development of the teachers they employ. As we will see later in this book, there has been a significant movement away from traditional HE-led teacher education, with a number of organisations such as Teach First and groups of schools now operating their own programmes. Whilst this process can be partly explained by the debate surrounding the relative importance of theory and practice, it is clear that the reform of teacher education is related to wider policy debates surrounding marketisation and choice. This has been mirrored in other parts of the public sector in the UK, especially England, and there has been a permanent revolution as policy continues to change (Hall, 2013).

However, despite the movement to the development of a market in education with choice and competition, there has been a paradox of increased central control over parts of the education system (Ball, 1994). For example, as we will show in later chapters, there has been increased quality control over teacher education in England, through national inspection by the Office for Standards in Education, Children's Services and Skills (Ofsted). Common standards set by central government for teacher education have been established (DfE, 2011). For schools, a whole range of restrictions have been placed on them by central government, including National Curriculum and assessment frameworks, and regular inspection based on national standards by Ofsted.

In reality, a completely free market has not been established in education and we have seen the development of a so-called 'quasi market' (Le Grand and Bartlett, 1993). Under this type of market there is limited competition with the state controlling entry to the market, imposing controls on curriculum and assessment and enforcing a national inspection framework. In England, within teacher education this scenario has been long established, as new organisations have been encouraged to provide a range of training routes. People who wish to train as a teacher therefore have a choice of routes and information is provided through inspection reports and various league tables. Providers who fail to recruit sufficient numbers or who fail to meet the required standards are allowed or encouraged to withdraw from the market. In teacher education, HE involvement has declined as new organisations such as Teach First or MATs such as Absolute Return for Kids have entered the market and developed alternative school-based teacher training programmes.

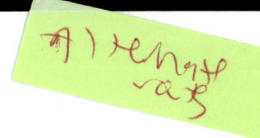

Political interference and the importance of education

The market-led approach in education has developed largely as a consequence of political pressure. A key component of this has been the perceived link between education and economic prosperity. Neoliberal policies were introduced in the 1980s as a response to the economic problems experienced in the previous decade. In the UK, successive governments implemented a succession of policies to deal with the perceived low standards in schools and to create a high-performing education system. There are a number of economic arguments for implementing policies that are designed to improve school standards:

- In a global economy, the UK must be able to effectively compete with other countries.
- Given the UK is not able to compete on the basis of cost due to the emergence of low-cost economies, we have to focus on ideas, innovation and high skill sectors (the so-called knowledge economy).
- To enable the UK to compete, standards in our schools have to be high and rising at least as fast as our competitors.
- The government has a responsibility to ensure that standards continue to rise in schools and colleges and to develop strategies and systems that produce skilled and motivated young people.
- This will involve major changes in the education system in order to maintain our level of economic competitiveness.
- A successful education system will produce young people who are able to make a positive contribution to the economic wellbeing of the country.
- A flexible and skilled workforce will enable the UK to successfully compete in a global economy. (Adapted from Abbott et al., 2013: 136–7)

Given the significance that education is perceived to play in dealing with economic realities, and the threats from global competition, it is hardly surprising that education has become a major political issue. Abbott (2015: 334) has argued that education 'has become an area of intense key political debate and a significant feature of the party manifesto and any subsequent General Election campaign'. Consequently, education has become more important as a policy area and there has been increasing interference by politicians, often at the expense of education professionals. A key feature of this is the drive to raise standards in schools, and in

England there has been ongoing curriculum and assessment reform, in addition to a whole range of policies relating to school organisation and funding that successive secretaries of state have introduced. Given that the quality of teaching is a major factor in determining pupil outcomes and raising standards, it is no surprise that policy reform should eventually focus on the way in which teachers are trained and their wider professional development.

We will return to look in detail at these policies in later chapters but it is worth considering some of the general themes that have emerged:

- Ensuring trainee teachers spend more time in school engaged in teaching and working with pupils.
- An increased role for schools and teachers in areas such as selection, supervision and assessment.
- An emphasis on high levels of subject knowledge for entrants.
- A decline in the amount of theory trainee teachers are exposed to during their training.
- A movement to teaching being seen as a vocational rather than a professional occupation.
- Identification of particular models of teaching and classroom management reducing the amount of experimentation and experience of alternative models.
- Centralised control of teacher education, with a defined curriculum and the imposition of national standards.
- A decline in the influence of HE institutions and their staff.
- A national system of inspection with publication of reports and the development of league tables.
- Problems of teacher retention, especially in certain schools.
- Encouragement for new and alternative providers to compete with existing institutions.
- Development of different models and routes to obtain qualified teacher status.
- The growth of political interference in teacher education policy and practice.

A number of countries, such as the United States, Australia and New Zealand, have experienced some of these developments, but the system in England has exemplified and magnified these trends. The rate of change has been significant and rapid, with teacher education being consistently under attack, especially from politicians of different political parties. What has emerged in England is a fragmented system, with schools now firmly at the centre of the training process. However, as we will see later in the book, schools and the teachers involved in teacher education do not completely accept some of the restrictions placed on the training of teachers. Many teachers take a more rounded view of the training process and are keen to develop a range of teaching models with due reference to educational theory and research. They often provide the trainees with whom they are working with a range of experiences that is at variance with the centrally directed curriculum. As Menter (2016: 11) has argued, 'there may be a strong cultural continuity across the teaching profession in the UK and indeed internationally, that is not reflected in the differences of political rhetoric in individual jurisdictions'.

Teacher autonomy

As part of the neoliberalisation agenda there has been a systematic attack on teacher autonomy in England. This has taken the form of increased standardisation of the curriculum, assessment and teaching methods employed in schools. Initially, this trend was focussed on serving teachers in schools, as successive governments sought to bring about change with the underlying focus being on raising standards in schools. However, teacher education soon also became a focus for these pressures. David Blunkett, secretary of state for education in the first New Labour government, quoted in Abbott et al. (2013: 138), summed up how a government seeks to transform the education system: 'We wanted to change standards, we needed leadership in schools, we needed high-quality teaching, we needed to revamp the materials, the equipment, the buildings that children are learning in, we needed to recruit first class teachers'.

A significant part of the drive to reduce teacher autonomy has been the rise of New Public Management (NPM) (see for example Hall, 2013). Middlewood and Abbott (2017: 7) have argued that 'NPM is a reflection of the reform of the public education system that embodies privatization, increased choice, performance management, use of private sector management approaches and greater accountability'. Through their introduction, these market-led reforms are intended to solve problems in the education system by placing a series of measures and expectations on the people working in the system. Autonomy is replaced by centralised control enforced through a series of performance measures and target setting. As a consequence of these developments, the ability of teachers to develop alternative strategies and for contextual factors to be taken into account has become more limited.

Initially applied to schools, this approach quickly became a feature of teacher education in England, as central government lost any trust in the existing models of teacher education. This has taken a number of forms, including, for example, specific guidance about how literacy should be developed through a particular approach, to the way in which children should be taught to read systematic synthetic phonics. This created a large amount of disquiet amongst teacher educators, who had previously been able to promote a range of reading schemes and to question the effectiveness of systematic synthetic phonics.

Trippestad, Swennen and Werler (2017: 9) have argued that 'the many waves of reforming teacher education have left teacher education with a diverse and complex struggle coming from both within the profession and the outside, challenging and restructuring traditional modes of teacher education work, identity and position'. The result of these pressures in England and to a lesser extent in many other parts of the world has been to create a crisis of confidence in teacher education. Progressive approaches to classroom practice have been replaced by a re-emergence of traditional teaching and assessment approaches. Target setting, performance management and a greater emphasis on outcomes rather than process have curtailed the ability of all teachers, but especially trainee teachers, to experiment and innovate.

The focus of teacher education

We will describe later in the book how the focus of teacher education in England has changed from being broadly a partnership between schools and HE, often with the agenda being set by HE, to becoming increasingly school-based. Is this an issue, and should there be any cause for concern about this shift of location? There is general agreement that in order to become a teacher a person needs to have first-hand experience of working in a school with young people. This experience is vital in developing the skills necessary to cope and survive in a classroom. However, there is an argument that all you need to become an effective teacher is to have good subject knowledge and practical experience of teaching. The shift of location of the training process to schools illustrates this belief.

We would argue that there is much more to becoming an effective teacher than gaining practical experience, however useful this might be. The ability to reflect, to make use of appropriate research and to experiment and sometimes to fail should all be part of the training process. Failure in a teaching context is a difficult concept, because the teacher is working with children and they have a right to effective teaching. However, often mistakes made by a teacher during their training can lead to improved performance, given time for guidance from an experienced member of staff and given appropriate reflection time. The pressure of an output-driven and performance-management system can make this difficult to achieve. Teaching is not a precise science and being allowed to develop a range of strategies in a safe and supportive environment is essential for professional development. Indeed, ongoing professional development should be at the heart of any teacher education programme. Therefore, a programme involving a number of different participants is required, even in a system increasingly dedicated to work in schools, to bring about successful outcomes for trainee teachers. This should include:

- The opportunity to study and analyse practice in single and double-loop terms, enabling a systematic analysis of the process (Brighouse, 1991).
- Learning from other staff, including everyday opportunities to talk with other colleagues at all levels. This should include informal observations in a range of schools and organisations.
- Specific provision including being mentored, appraised or formally observed during teaching practice. Being given the opportunity of understudying staff or a particular post. Also the opportunity to attend specific seminars, workshops, conferences or structured visits to other organisations.
- External provision, including HE-based, in addition to meeting staff and trainee teachers from other institutions and age phases.
- The opportunity for personal reading, reflection and study. (Adapted from Middlewood and Abbott, 2015: 11)

Given this mixed-methods approach, we would argue that teacher educators have a key role to play in the initial training and subsequent professional development of teachers. However, as we will explain later in the book, their role has had to change and adapt to the new realities of teacher education that have emerged over the last 30 years in England.

Technicians or professionals?

A significant feature of the debate in England compared to many other parts of the world has been the shift from seeing teaching as a profession to it being considered as a technical activity. In Chapter 6 we will consider some of the alternative approaches adopted in other countries. The most striking example is in Finland, which has adopted a strong university-based system that is in almost total opposition to the school-led system being developed in England. As part of the movement to this school-led system, there has also been a strong emphasis on the necessity of trainee teachers to acquire a specific set of skills, which can then be assessed against sets of skills or capabilities (Ball, 2003b and Brown et al., 2014). This development has been at the expense of traits such as reflection, a commitment to social justice and the use of research to develop policy and classroom practice. The reduced emphasis on these traits has resulted in teacher education becoming increasingly one dimensional, as teachers are trained to reproduce particular approaches and achieve targeted outcomes. Diversity across programmes has been reduced, but trainee teachers are able to choose between a range of different routes and providers.

Teachers do need to possess a range of basic skills to be able to deliver effective lessons to their pupils. In any training programme there is a clear need to develop a good range of classroom practices to create a positive learning environment. There are certain methods, approaches and skills that all teachers need to learn and to put into practice. However, teachers also need the skills to be able to develop and adapt to particular classes, individuals and situations. Teaching is not a precise science (Brant and Vincent, 2017). Certain skills and methods can be developed and good practice embedded into classroom practice. However, crucial to this process is the ability to be able to reflect on practice and to learn from what has gone before.

'Good' teaching

If we are going to consider the ways in which teachers are going to be trained, it is important to attempt to arrive at a definition of what is good teaching. Are there certain common characteristics that can be taught to create good teachers? What constitutes good teaching and what are the characteristics of good teachers? Brant and Vincent (2017: 171) argue that good teaching 'is a highly skilled, dynamic and creative process that involves utilizing a whole range of different types of knowledge and acquired professional expertise'. There have been a number of attempts to identify a good teacher and good teaching (see for example DfEE 2000; Turner-

Bissett, 2001; Coe et al., 2014; Middlewood and Abbott, 2015). A number of common features have emerged, including:

- subject knowledge;
- effective pedagogy;
- classroom climate, including teacher expectations and the interaction between teacher and pupil;
- time management;
- effective classroom management with clarity and consistency of rules that are effectively enforced;
- effective questioning and the use of assessment for learning;
- professional development;
- support given to colleagues; and
- communication with stakeholders, including parents.

To many, especially those outside education, the impact on the pupils' ability to learn and to ultimately achieve certain outcomes is the true measure of how effective a teacher is and, in simplistic terms, whether they are good or not. However, anyone with classroom experience can confirm that in practice, a complex number of factors will contribute to good or improving pupil outcomes. The quality of the teacher and teaching is important, but the relationship between the quality of teaching and pupil outcomes is complex and often difficult to isolate. Trying to identify good teachers and teaching is not as straightforward as it may appear. However, there are a number of elements that we have identified above, which can contribute to the development of a range of practices that will enable good teaching to take place and create good teachers.

It is difficult to isolate individual characteristics but the three conceptualisations put forward by Moore (2004) may be useful in determining what elements are required to develop a good teacher. He argues that the first is the 'saviour teacher': this is the teacher often portrayed by the media who through the force of their personality is able to get pupils to buy into their methods and enable pupils to succeed. Personality, enthusiasm, love of the subject, high expectations and interest in the pupils are all factors that will enable this 'natural' teacher to succeed. Second, there is the 'competent craftsperson' who can acquire the skills to deliver effective lessons from working with more experienced teachers. They learn what methods work and how to maximise their personal strengths. Over a period of time this person develops the strategies to teach effective lessons and to meet the competencies that are required to become an effective teacher. This would involve developing a technical approach to teaching that can be replicated over different schools and classrooms. Finally, Moore identifies the 'reflective practitioner' who will reflect on their own practice to bring about self-improvement. This will be supported by making use of educational research, in addition to careful evaluation and drawing on a range of techniques and experiences.

For most teachers, the reality is that they will combine all three of the characteristics set out above. They will need to be enthusiastic and to display a love of their subject, allied to developing a range of skills that will be necessary to produce effective lessons. They will then need to reflect on their practice to bring about ongoing improvement. During their training teachers should bring an enthusiasm for their subject and develop certain skills necessary to succeed in the classroom, with opportunities for self-reflection on their practice. Different models of teacher education will emphasise different aspects of this process, but perhaps the best model of teacher education will provide opportunities for a full range of experience and meet the needs of a range of trainee teachers who will go on to become 'good' teachers.

Conclusion

Having established some of the general trends that have influenced teacher education, we will go on to consider in detail some of the specific policies that have been implemented. This book will focus on teacher education in England but will also look at the debate around teacher education in a number of other countries. In England, the policy changes relating to teacher education have been part of a broader agenda, designed to revolutionise the wider education system drawing on so-called free-market principles. Therefore, we will attempt to place the changes to teacher education in a broader context of educational policy reform.

The emphasis, from successive governments, has been to raise standards in schools and to ensure that the English school system is amongst the best in the world. Ensuring high-quality teachers who are able to deliver high-quality lessons to their pupils will be at the heart of this process. No one would disagree with the intention to raise standards and to ensure schools have the best possible teachers who are able to teach outstanding lessons. However, how this is achieved is open to debate and the methods and systems employed will be of interest to a number of stakeholders. Increasingly, schools and their serving teachers are playing a more significant role in the training of teachers, as there is an increased focus on classroom practice at the expense of theory. In Chapter 2 we will begin to explore how the training of teachers was initially conceived and influenced by wider policy initiatives and the way in which teacher education responded to the pressures it had to deal with.

2

THE EARLY DAYS OF TEACHER TRAINING

Introduction

This chapter begins by considering briefly how the earliest ideas about education came to influence present-day practices in teacher training. It notes how in the United Kingdom (UK) and elsewhere the majority of children had no formal teaching at all until the nineteenth century. Even when universal education was perceived to be desirable and more extensive provision was made for schools, the teachers were seldom trained and often they were not even expected to have received much education themselves.

The pre-1900 debate about types of training and the eventual involvement of the government in teacher training is briefly considered and the chapter examines the earliest 'apprenticeship' models of teacher training and compares them briefly with other models being developed at the time, both in other European countries and at various centres in the UK. The impact of the Great War, 1914–18, and the subsequent progress in initial teacher training between the wars, is considered before the chapter moves on to consider the intense debate on education in general and teacher training in particular during and after the Second World War. The McNair Report (1944) and its influence on the Education Act 1944 is considered in detail, as is the Emergency Training Scheme (ETS) for teachers which began in 1943. The following years of rapid expansion in initial teacher training are considered along with the implications for initial teacher training, of selection of pupils for grammar schools at age 11, the Crowther Report (DES, 1959) and moves towards an all-graduate profession. The chapter ends with brief reference to the Robbins Report (DES, 1963b), which is then considered in greater detail in Chapter 3. Throughout this chapter, three institutions which are illustrative of the developments taking place during the period are cited to demonstrate differing examples of teacher training institutions:

- Canley College Coventry was part of the ETS in 1943 and became a teacher training college in 1948. It was merged with the University of Warwick in 1978.
- St Mary's College Cheltenham was founded as a church institution midway through the nineteenth century and has only recently become part of a university.
- The University of Worcester was an RAF station at the end of the Second World War. Emergency teacher training started there after the war in an institution that became a university in its own right in 2005.

Education for all

For Bertrand Russell (1946), it was the tendency towards democracy of early liberalism – and the belief that all men are born equal – which led to education being seen as an important factor in the development of all children, and not just those of the upper classes. The gradual acceptance that knowledge and learning were not confined to the established church or other prevailing orthodoxies meant that in the UK in the late Victorian era, serious thought was being given to how people should be educated and to the role of the state in their education. Questions about the teaching of children, the nature of learning and what should be taught automatically followed. This in turn led to consideration of who should teach the children, how these teachers should be recruited and how they ought to be trained.

These questions about learning and teaching meant that educational ideas taken initially from Aristotle and Plato formed part of an ongoing debate developed in the seventeenth and eighteenth centuries by Locke, Rousseau and others. This was continued in more recent times by, for example, Dewey (1916), Tawney (1914, 1931) and Peters (1959) and has become increasingly politicised in the twentieth and twenty-first centuries.

Teacher training in its infancy

The education of young people has a fundamental part to play in the organisation of every modern society. The training of teachers is a cornerstone of this process. Although this book attempts to analyse in detail the transformation of teacher training in the UK from the immediate post-war period to the present day, it is necessary initially to review teacher training in the period prior to 1944, since it was during the preceding 150 years that many procedures and processes in modern-day training were first tried and evaluated both in the UK and other parts of Europe.

This book is not simply confined to a chronology of events, acts of parliament and white papers but will also analyse the reasons for this legislation, the wider debate and the context at the time. Thus, changes in the school curriculum content reflect changes in contemporary society's view of what was important to that society. For example, science and technology, which are considered important factors in the modern world, have expanded, whereas arts and music are becoming marginalised and subjects such as home economics have been left out of the statutory curriculum. Some schools teach Chinese and Urdu because of the increasing involvement of Western society with China and because of the influx of children whose mother tongue is not English.

The idea of education as 'education for education's sake' to enhance personal development has largely been overtaken by a view of education as a tool to assist economic growth in society and to provide students with the means to acquire jobs. Since all these changes impact on the school curriculum, they not only influence the teaching of pupils but also the training of teachers.

Such developments might be expected in a modern society, but in the eighteenth and nineteenth centuries changes in the structure of society were regarded with suspicion and if change happened at all it was marginal. The predominant view held about children and their teachers was quite different from the modern perception and hence ideas about the education of children and teachers were vastly different from those pertaining today. Many people are familiar with the popular literature of the eighteenth and nineteenth centuries which caricatures 'educators' as being like Mr Squeers in *Nicholas Nickleby* by Charles Dickens. In addition, there are numerous instances in Jane Austin and elsewhere of the daughters of families who had fallen upon hard times becoming untrained governesses who 'educated' the daughters and sons of wealthy landowners. Likewise, village parsons often taught local children both as a means of bringing them into the church and to supplement inadequate stipends paid to local clergy.

Before 1800 the children of the general population were scarcely educated at all, although the Society for Promoting Christian Knowledge was founded in 1698 to help spread Christianity in charity schools and by 1821 the *Manchester Guardian*'s initial edition noted the 'great diffusion of Education within the last quarter of a century' (2017). Such teachers as existed were not trained as teachers. When the 1833 Reform Act raised awareness of the benefits to all of the education of working people, the idea that teachers would need to be recruited and properly trained was given more serious consideration. Thus, the formal training of teachers is a comparatively recent phenomenon across the world, as are the debates about who should do it and how it should be accomplished.

Following general acceptance of the idea that education should be for all, the government in the UK took a more centralising role in education via a series of education acts between 1868 and the end of the century (e.g. the Education Act (1870), the so called Forster's Act). These included involvement in aspects of teacher training, particularly with regard to funding. Various systems of training were already in evidence in Holland, Switzerland, France and Germany and these systems had a significant impact on many of the developments in Britain.

At the end of the nineteenth century some influential educational practitioners in Britain modelled their schoolteaching work on individual European pioneers such as Froebel, Montessori and Pestalozzi. They felt that their 'revolutionary' teaching methods ought to be reflected in the training given to students who wished to become teachers (Rich, 1933). Charlotte Mason was one such pioneer who tried to put this into practice because she felt that all children, regardless of social class, should have experience of a breadth of learning (Cholmondeley, 1960).

In Britain, the original teacher training institutions were founded in the middle of the nineteenth century by bodies such as the church and charities. One of the first in England was a training college or 'normal' school founded in Battersea in London in 1840, but there was a similar institution in Scotland which was founded some years earlier – the Glasgow Normal Seminary – where a lengthy debate about splitting the academic side of training from the professional continued for several years.

Models of training and the involvement of institutions

A model of training had been developed in England which relied on a kind of apprenticeship model in a 'normal' school in which pupil teachers worked under the guidance of experienced teachers before going on to work in other schools. This built upon the 'monitorial' system where older students monitored their younger counterparts. Although there are differences, it is worth comparing this approach to recent developments in teacher education. In the years between 1800 and 1840 some basic research evidence had been accumulated, which reported that such an approach was ineffective – for example in the National School Society reports of the period (Rich, 1933). As a result, consideration was given to the need for teachers to study a 'science of education' which would make them familiar with how the principles of psychology and philosophy related to the teaching of children. This would allow teachers to have insights into how children learn (Craig, 1843, quoted in Rich, 1933: 54). It was suggested that this notion of training, involving a professional element supplemented by an academic strand, ought to be based in universities where the academic work would be carried out. The professional or practical element would continue to be provided by schools.

However, the universities were not very interested in developing this approach (Rich, 1933). A somewhat different approach was pioneered at the Battersea Normal School (later Battersea Training College) in London, where the notion of teaching as a vocation was encouraged – following ideas taken from the training of teachers abroad, for example in Holland, Germany and France (Rich, 1933).

In spite of this somewhat rudimentary 'research' from the National School, support continued for the notion of an 'apprenticeship' in a 'normal' school being the only necessary basis for the training of elementary schoolteachers, provided that candidates were themselves well educated and had good subject knowledge.

Other institutions of the same period, for example the Home and Colonial School Society, followed the same general philosophy as Battersea, but the emphasis was on infant teaching – seen at the time as the province of women.

It was at the Home and Colonial School Society that Charlotte Mason taught before beginning her own college in Ambleside in the Lake District in 1892, where some of her more 'enlightened' ideas were employed (Cholmondly, 1960).

It had been accepted from an early stage that trained women were needed as well as men to become teachers. Thus, Bishop Otter Teacher Training College was founded in Lincoln in 1839 to train schoolmasters, and later began to accept women. In the 1870s the London-based Maria Grey Teacher Training and Registration Society began training women teachers for teaching in secondary schools. St Mary's College in Cheltenham was another example of an institution founded by the Church of England in 1847 which began to train women teachers.

The Church saw such institutions as an opportunity to become involved in the education of the working population. The original Cheltenham Training School was for women only, although it was set up in conjunction with a men's establishment. It was one of five such colleges set up by the church in this period and at the outset had 12 pupil teachers, who enrolled for between one month and three years depending on their previous background. In the early days a monitorial/apprenticeship model was used at St Mary's, as students in training worked in a 'normal' school but combined a substantial amount of academic work in the college. The numbers quickly grew to around 70, although science laboratories and library facilities were not available for another 70 years.

In the early days the syllabus here, as elsewhere, aimed to train teachers to prepare pupils to be good servants and industrial labourers – but included penmanship, arithmetic and domestic economy (Rich, 1933; Challinor, 1978).

Church attendance was compulsory for students at St Mary's as was religious studies. However, by 1870 the curriculum had developed to include history, geography, grammar, method of teaching and reading. By the end of the nineteenth century ancient languages and French were being taught to students, who were now able to study for a degree.

The debate involving educationalists and politicians about the need for professional and/or academic training was as fierce as it had been on the continent 60 years previously and as strident as it is has been recently in England (Becher, 1992). In 1897 a Training of Teachers Joint Committee (Rich, 1933) was set up to collect evidence on this question and advocated that there should be both strands in the training. Practice in teaching needed to be accompanied by an academic knowledge of the philosophy and sociology of education along with psychology, school organisation and the history of education. By 1900 this 'academic' work was included in work being carried out in 21 universities. However, although increasing numbers of teachers were needed throughout the later half of the nineteenth century, government financing fell well short of what was required (Challinor, 1978), with colleges like St Mary's receiving most of their funding from religious societies.

1897–1939: central government gets involved

The Education Act of 1899 led to the formation of a Board of Education to oversee education in the UK. Eventually, in 1906, a national register of teachers was set up showing the date of registration, qualifications and experience – a register which showed evidence of people who had started teaching up to 30 years previously. The 1902 Education Act set up local education authorities (LEAs) which were allowed to support training colleges in order to supplement the universities which trained aspiring teachers. It was accepted that many more teachers were needed and a serious effort was made to improve their training.

The monitorial/apprenticeship methods were criticised in the 1902 Act and curriculum and exams were now set by the Board of Education. Aspiring teachers were now required to have received a secondary education up to the age of 16. Serious consideration was given in the act to the teaching of infant-age children. The Dyke Report in 1906 (Rich, 1933) recommended that good elementary teachers were needed who were interested in science and technology and that training colleges should offer appropriate courses.

The 1918 Education Act (the Fisher Act) consolidated many of these developments as the country came to terms with the implications of a post-war society. The school leaving age was raised from 12 to 14, thus increasing the need for more recruits to the teaching profession, and LEAs were charged with ensuring that children below the age of 12 were not allowed to be employed. There was an abolition of school fees in state schools and the introduction of inspections and attendance registers. As a result of earlier concerns about the fitness of service recruits for the 1914 war, physical education and health education were seen as important additions to the curriculum.

The years between 1918 and 1939 saw an extended period of economic depression, during which the school leaving age was raised to 15 for most children. However, the teacher training numbers were cut nationally to save money as part of ongoing reductions in public expenditure. This was a difficult time financially for colleges, but in other respects progress was being made. For example, in Cheltenham, St Mary's College separated entirely from the men's college but continued with its work and in the 1930s became involved in the Training College Association, an organisation set up to consider the methods used in preparing teachers for work in infant and junior schools (Challinor, 1978).

The association considered that psychology, sociology and child studies ought to be regarded as important subjects for all students and consequently they were developed in the curricula of most training colleges.

Several reports on education were published in the years leading up to 1939, for example the Hadow Reports (Board of Education, 1933) and the Spens Report (Board of Education, 1938). They contributed to the hugely significant 1944 Education Act which was implemented at the end of the Second World War.

Sir William Hadow was an educationalist whose work was built upon by Lady Plowden three decades later (see Chapter 3), when producing her significant report into primary education. Hadow believed that schools ought not to be places of compulsory instruction but of cooperation, in which the curriculum gave opportunity for experiences to be developed and creativity allowed to flourish; a curriculum in which the main aim was not only to learn dry facts for regurgitation but also allowed aesthetic development to occur. Influenced by writers and psychologists such as Dewey, Montessori, McMillan and Isaacs, consideration was given to aspects of childhood which were far removed from earlier 'Victorian' ideas of how children ought to be educated (Galton et al., 1980). Tawney (1931), writing in the same vein, remarked on the benefit of suiting the curriculum and educational methods to individual needs as a result of increased knowledge of psychology. These ideas were taken up and propagated throughout training colleges during the inter-war period.

War years

During the 1939–45 war, there was a good deal of debate about what education provision there should be following the end of the war. There was an intention to give those who had fought and those who had suffered a better future, and to use social policy to ensure there was no return to the problems of the inter-war period. There were echoes here of the intentions after the First World War, which for some at least were not translated into political action after 1918. A white paper in 1943 – 'Education Reconstruction' (Board of Education, 1943) – proposed that after the war the school leaving age be raised to 15 years for all children and that the previous system of elementary education be changed to a tripartite system, so that schools could become primary and secondary, followed by the possibility of further education. The age of transfer from primary to secondary was proposed to be set at age 11 years. Provision was to be standardised across the country and education was to be free, with LEAs having increased responsibilities in this field.

The McNair Report (Board of Education, 1944)

R.A. Butler was a Conservative politician who held a post in the Cabinet as president of the Board of Education in 1941. He appointed a committee to consider how the supply, recruitment methods and training of teachers and youth leaders should be carried out after the war. The chair was Arnold McNair and under his guidance the committee produced proposals in 1944, whilst the Education Act was going through Parliament.

The white paper, 'Education Reconstruction' (para 100), welcomed the fact that the recruitment and training of teachers was being dealt with in the McNair Report. It lamented the poor quality of teachers and suggested some reasons. Among them the fact that most teachers were recruited from grammar schools whereas only a small proportion of the pupils they were teaching had any likelihood of experiencing selective education. Teachers were seen to need a wider experience of life than simply working in schools. Poor salaries were also blamed, although the accepted practices of paying women less than men and having women retire upon marriage were not to change for many years.

A significant debating point within the McNair committee was whether teacher training ought to be in the hands of the universities or of area training authorities (ATAs), which would be responsible for ensuring that adequate training facilities existed across the country. Eventually, there was agreement that a central training council should be set up to advise the Board of Education on setting up these ATAs. Other proposals were that schools would have a deputy headteacher as well as a headteacher and that teachers would have a basic 'qualified teacher status' with salary scales that rewarded special qualifications and experience. Existing pay scales were regarded as too low and in need of substantial improvement.

There was concern about how to attract new recruits to the profession. Older men and women were needed as well as younger people, but specific qualifications were to be demanded of those coming into teaching at a young age. Such aspiring teachers ought to be educated up to 18 years of age and then have three more years training to become a teacher. Graduates should have extra training after their degree course. It was further suggested that courses in teacher training include an element of teaching practice in a suitable school, tuition in English for all and specialist tuition for teachers of arts and crafts, music, physical education and domestic subjects. For teachers in further education the need for cooperation with industry and commerce was noted.

The ATAs would be given the responsibility of overseeing the assessment of students in the light of requirements set out by the Board of Education. Furthermore, the committee recommended that the Board of Education should establish a research council to enable the study of aspects of education such as childhood and adolescence.

The McNair Committee recommendations highlighted the problems of teacher supply which would be caused by the reorganisation of the structure of education provision in the UK and the raising of the school leaving age, but urged that any central control of the training of teachers be avoided. The dangers inherent within the centralisation of power and authority in the training of teachers was particularly highlighted.

The Emergency Training Scheme

Significant development as a result of the McNair report did not occur until after the end of the war, but an ETS for teachers was introduced by the wartime coalition government in 1943, when it became obvious that there were not enough suitably qualified teachers. The scheme was supported after the war by the Labour government of Clement Atlee and his minister of education, Ellen Wilkinson. Men and women were recruited from the services to complete an intensive training course of one year in a college followed by two years of probation. No formal academic requirements were necessary and the scheme was immediately successful in terms of recruitment. A thousand applicants per week were received at the outset and eventually 37,000 were accepted (Vernon, 1982).

This influx led inevitably to problems of accommodation, staffing, administration and placement in the colleges. Many problems were overcome by Ellen Wilkinson's dogged support of the policy, and 35,000 teachers were trained before the scheme ended in 1951.

In Canley in Coventry, an industrial workers' hostel which could house up to 1,000 people was commandeered and served for training nearly 500 prospective teachers. It was used for that purpose until 1947 and then became part of a permanent teacher training college which subsequently became part of the University of Warwick (Abbott, 2008).

At Worcester, a wartime RAF base was subject to a 'Hut Operation for the Raising of the School Leaving Age' (Vernon, 1982) and quickly became one of the 55 similarly commandeered centres. The buildings at Worcester, which resembled a barracks, were turned into college facilities for 240 demobilised servicemen and women who began training there in 1946. Problems abounded at all the colleges because of food rationing, transport difficulties and the shortages caused by the war, though these were commonplace throughout the country and in all walks of life. It is noted in Cheesewright (2008) that the students were less rigidly disciplined than in the armed forces. They were not required to have previous qualifications and thus had to study every subject they would teach in addition to techniques of classroom practice.

Existing colleges like St Mary's College in Cheltenham also contributed to alleviating the post-war shortage of teachers. When the war started in 1939 the college had been evacuated to Wales for a short period but returned to Cheltenham, even though the buildings were bombed. The McNair Committee visited in 1942 as part of their task to prepare a plan for the development of teacher training after the war. In 1944 the college participated in the ETS and numbers rose to 300 (Challinor, 1978).

The Education Training Scheme did not, however, completely solve the problem of teacher supply, for it was predicted that 200,000 teachers would be needed by 1948. Ellen Wilkinson, the minister, supported the ideal of free education for all and was enthusiastic to raise the school leaving age to 15 as advocated in the 1944 Education Act (Vernon, 1982). This led inevitably to an increased requirement for teachers suitably qualified to teach in the new tripartite system (Abbott et al, 2013; Cheesewright, 2008). Numbers more than doubled in the next decade and accommodation was increased accordingly. Teaching facilities in colleges improved to include specialist buildings such as gymnasia, laboratories, libraries and teaching rooms.

1944–50

The implementation of the 1944 Education Act by the Labour Party led to the setting up of two central advisory councils, one for England and one for Wales. Responsibility for education was divided between LEAs, teachers and the Board of Education, which, in the Act, became the Ministry of Education. The ministry had greater power than the defunct board. As McNair had suggested, the act gave teachers control of the curriculum and teaching methods. They were officially encouraged to think for themselves and formulate their own teaching methods; uniformity was to be frowned upon. The act accepted the need for the primary/secondary/further division of schooling – a tripartite system – which gave rise to a selective test at 11 (the 11-plus) (Abbott et al., 2013). The school leaving age was raised and headteachers were to be allowed to set school policies and manage resources. The LEAs were urged to contribute to the training of teachers and had a responsibility to 'establish, maintain and assist training colleges' (para 62).

In 1949, the National Advisory Council on the Training and Supply of Teachers was set up to advise on a national policy for the training, qualification and supply of teachers. Thirteen ATAs were set up and by 1950 over 50 new training colleges had opened and another 70 soon followed. The universities continued their training programmes and in many instances initiated schools of education as advocated in the McNair Report. There was a concern before the war that the type of training colleges for teachers had become so diverse that staff were isolated and there was little interaction between tutors who were engaged in the same profession (Challinor, 1978; Cheesewright, 2008). Schools of education in universities allowed expertise to be shared in studies such as 'The Theory and Practice of Education' and the supervision of teaching practice. Colleges were encouraged to develop different specialist courses – at St Mary's, for example, needlework, art, religious education, science and physical education.

In 1947 St Mary's, Cheltenham became associated with the University of Bristol, along with eight other local institutions – an example of an individual institution bringing long experience of teacher training into an embryonic national system. The university with which the college was associated was responsible for the examination of students and the award of their qualification.

The City of Coventry Training College, on the other hand, was a good example of the type of institution set up by a local authority at the conclusion of the ETS. The premises used by the ETS were taken over by the LEA, which originally planned a mixed college. However, there was a pressing need for women to train as infant teachers, so in September 1948 the college started a two-year training course for women. Men were not enrolled until 1958 (Abbott, 2008). A government grant was available for the building, equipment and maintenance costs, but to begin with the college was housed entirely on the premises of the emergency training courses. However, the final ETS course was not completed until December 1948, so the autumn 1948 term of the women's course was spent in the student's home areas, observing schools and doing some teaching. When the new intake of 180 arrived in Coventry in January 1949, they were taught by six male staff who had taught on the emergency course. The staff numbers quickly increased to over 20, with qualifications ranging from training diplomas to degrees and doctorates. The premises were initially in a poor state, but the Coventry LEA intended to rebuild the site. The academic curriculum in 1948 included health and hygiene, rural studies, needlework and education, as well as those subjects which are part of the curriculum today. On teaching practice, whole-class teaching was expected to be the norm, sometimes in schools with classes of up to 60 in deprived areas of Coventry. Students on practice were welcomed by the schools who appreciated the exposure to education theory brought about by involvement with the college (Abbott, 2008).

Living in college, students were expected to conform to the ethos of the times in dress code and general behaviour. These values were expected to be passed on to their pupils in the schools. Men and women were often in separate colleges or in separate buildings within a college. They ate in communal dining halls with staff at a high table. Visiting times were strictly enforced, particularly for male visitors to the rooms of female students. Weekend passes were difficult to obtain, especially as some colleges had lectures on Saturday mornings. In church colleges, students were expected to attend services on Sundays. (These conditions applied in some colleges until well into the 1960s.) Students at Coventry studied to teach particular age ranges, with the emphasis being determined by the national need. University affiliation was initially with the University of Birmingham and their Institute of Education, although this changed when the University of Warwick was founded in 1965.

In 1948, on completion of the ETS, the Ministry of Education invited the Institution in Worcester to become the City of Worcester Training College and continue with the training of teachers. It too became a college associated with the University of Birmingham, with a two-year course for the qualification of the Certificate of Education. Their specialities were to be rural studies and domestic science taught to a mixed body of students.

Expansion

In the 1951 general election a Conservative government under Winston Churchill was elected. Initially, Churchill determined to cut educational spending because of the country's dire economic situation. Education was not seen as a priority and some Conservatives reportedly still doubted the wisdom of the policy of free education for all (Gillard, 2011). However, the post-war increase in the birth rate meant that by 1955 it was a political necessity to train an increasing number of infant teachers. The minister of education was not seen as a desirable job in government and two ministers, Viscount Hailsham and David Eccles, both held the post in a short period. There is little evidence that the ministers had much interest or influence in the department (Abbott et al., 2013) although Viscount Hailsham advocated an extension in the length of teacher training courses.

Gradually, however, it was accepted that by raising the standard of education the long-term interests of the country would be served. A rise in educational standards and a better-educated work force ought to contribute to a more productive economy. Spending therefore increased, although the differences in provision between selective schools and others was very marked, especially in the teacher/pupil ratio. Many state primary schools and secondary modern schools had inadequate buildings, outside toilets, poor or non-existent playing fields and a shortage of staff. Towards 1960, when Harold Macmillan became prime minister, there was a growing awareness of the corrosive influences of inequalities arising from the selective nature of education and particularly the 11-plus exam (Kogan, 1987).

Selection at age 11

The 11-plus exam was a means of selection which pupils sat in their final year of primary school. This led to competition between primary schools to get children ready for the exam. As a result, the curriculum in primary schools was often narrow and streaming was practised to segregate children into '11-plus' streams and the 'others'. In different parts of the country the varying size of population and number of grammar schools that existed created a situation where proportionally different numbers of children were selected by the 11-plus. For example, in rural East Anglia three times more were selected than in the City of Birmingham. Across the country there was a policy of selecting more boys than girls for an academic education (Abbott et al., 2013).

As living standards rose, people became aware of the importance of the individual natures and needs of their children, which for a large proportion of the population were not being met. Pressure grew to train more teachers, make schools more comprehensive and to defer selection. Thus, for example, in 1957 in Leicestershire selection was deferred until 14, with all children first going to a high school at 11 years of age. Sir David Eccles, who was a minister of education twice between 1954 and 1962, was credited with making persuasive arguments to increase education expenditure in order to improve educational standards across the population (Abbott et al., 2013). In pursuance of this he was happy to approve the creation of a more 'comprehensive' type of school in some areas of the country, as he saw the need for a fairer, more broadly based educational system. These developments meant that training institutions needed to take more trainees and teach them to cope with different challenges arising from mixed-ability classes of older children and various types of 'middle school' age groups.

The Crowther Report

In the early years of his tenure, David Eccles asked Sir Geoffrey Crowther to chair a committee charged with considering the education of children between the ages of 15 and 19 in a modern industrial society. Geoffrey Crowther had experience as a journalist and economist who had worked in the government during the war. In 1956 he had been appointed as chair of the Central Advisory Council for Education. The Crowther Report (DES, 1959) considered the balance of education for these pupils. It was founded upon careful research and the recommendations were wide ranging.

The report noted (para 3) that a shortage of teachers was a considerable hindrance to economic progress and that implementation of the committee's recommendations would depend to a large extent on an expansion of the teaching force. In para 625, it emphasised that progress in education depended on having teachers with the right qualities and in the right numbers. More teachers were required to bring down class sizes to a desirable ratio of 1:17 – especially when the school leaving age was raised. The committee's view was that classes were generally too large.

In addition, the report pointed out that improving the quality of education for the whole school population would increase the pool from which well-educated recruits to teaching would eventually come. Disappointment was expressed that the numbers of graduates going into teaching had previously been so low and that the standard of education of training college recruits, who gained teaching certificates, was not of sufficient quality. This problem, the report suggested, could be countered by the typically two-year certificate course becoming a three-year course.

The committee also highlighted the fact that the schools which had most difficulty recruiting teachers were in areas of social deprivation and were those in which the task of teaching was most difficult. Unfortunately, that meant that in many instances new and inexperienced teachers found themselves employed in the most challenging situations and there was 'a kill or cure initiation' (para 629). There was a detailed study of the routes of initial training in colleges and universities. It referred in para 451 to the issue of attracting school pupils to a career in teaching and noted that many more girls than boys were likely to go to training colleges to train and that it was possible to enter training college with lower levels of qualification than to enter university (in which more boys were likely to study). It welcomed the flexibility of college courses, through which most primary schoolteachers were trained, because in addition to specialist subjects, all primary teachers needed knowledge of music, art, crafts and physical education – all of which were included in the college training. Crowther noted, however, that mathematics, another essential subject for primary teachers, was often not routinely included in training courses.

These factors reinforced his view that academic standards ought not to be set too high in colleges since schools needed those who had a 'gift' for knowing and teaching young children as much as subject knowledge. However, he saw the difficulty of getting some sixth formers to consider training to teach this variety of subjects as additions to their specialisms – subjects which they may have given up many years previously.

The report argued strongly (para 658) that the number of prospective teachers trained through the college system must be increased, to cope with the increased pupil numbers which would be caused by raising the school leaving age – which he advocated occur sometime between 1965 and 1969 (para 674) (this eventually happened in 1972) and the post-war increase in birth rate (the so-called bulge).

Crowther also recommended that the increase in teacher numbers be achieved by campaigning to attract older people and university graduates to the profession. As a corollary to this, the material rewards and working conditions for the teaching profession needed improvement. Flexibility in pay needed to take account of the need for specialist staff in sixth forms and the difficulty of recruiting staff in what he called 'bad' areas of the country (para 693).

Moves towards an all-graduate profession

An expansion of the teaching force was approved in 1959, when David Eccles was also advised by the National Advisory Council on the Training and Supply of Teachers that 16,000 new teachers were required. As mentioned earlier, this advisory body had been set up pre-1950 to study the processes of training and supply and to advise the minister. In the context of individual institutions throughout the 1950s, two common themes are clearly apparent:

1. Certificate courses were lengthened from two to three years and included education studies.
2. The colleges were expanded to accept increased numbers of trainee teachers.

The intention of the former was to make a better-educated teaching force with a view to eventually having an all-graduate teaching profession. Changes to academic programmes were therefore instituted in virtually all colleges throughout the country. For example, Canley in Coventry had a two-year certificate course for primary teachers validated by Birmingham University, with students studying a main subject and a combined subsidiary such as music and movement. This became a three-year course in 1960. Worcester College was required to have rural studies and domestic science as specialist subjects for 20 per cent of their 360 students – also validated by Birmingham University. The new certificate course was broken down into a three-year specialism, with a second subject studied for two years. Teaching practice of 14 weeks was spread throughout the course. The college also began to take students aiming to teach in secondary modern schools. St Mary's in Cheltenham offered religious education as one specialism and introduced some teaching practice placements in distant schools with the students lodging away from college, in cities like Birmingham and Swindon. The last two-year course started in 1959 and this was replaced by a three-year certificate.

Education studies was seen as an important component of all courses, as the certificate became seen as a preliminary stage in formulating the four-year bachelor of education. Education studies might be conceived as having started in the 1930s, when the Training College Association considered that psychology, sociology and child studies ought to be in the curriculum of training colleges. References to this in various guises can be found in the records of the experiences of students at the time and in contemporary curriculum documents (Abbott, 2008; Cheesewright, 2008).

In 1948, the curriculum at Canley included an aspiration to encourage students to try out a wide variety of teaching methods in the Coventry schools. Students also studied the 1944 Education Act. The schools in Coventry were said to be pleased to be linked to 'the progressive educational thought of a training college' (Abbott, 2008).

At St Mary's, the study of education had been deemed to be helpful in the late 1940s (Challinor, 1978). At Worcester, staff are recorded as wrestling with the relationship of theory and practice of education in the courses for 1954 (Cheesewright, 2008).

Education studies has always attracted polarised views (Lawlor, 1990; Woods, 1972), but was regarded as vital to an aspiring teacher, until constant criticism of the content of teacher training from a hostile media and press led to a rethink during the 1970s. The study of education studies then became anathema to the Conservative government led by Margaret Thatcher in the 1980s (Abbott et al., 2013). Further consideration of education studies will be included in the following chapters.

The numbers of trainees in the colleges during this decade increased rapidly, largely because of errors in the predictions of the school population. Government figures had originally predicted that the school population was going to decline in the early 1960s. This predicted fall in pupil numbers was soon found to be inaccurate (Cheesewright, 2008) and led to an expected shortfall of thousands of teachers (Challinor, 1978). Consequently, colleges were required to take 4,000 extra trainee teachers. In Canley, over the ten-year period numbers doubled to 400 and in Worcester the 350-strong student body of 1958 became 550 by 1962. St Mary's increased from 350 to 550 students. These increases were mirrored in all colleges across the UK and accompanied by vigorous building programmes of accommodation and facilities.

The colleges were still coping with these ongoing expansion programmes when, in the early 1960s, the Conservative government announced the setting up of an enquiry under Lord Robbins (DES, 1963b) to examine the whole of full-time higher education in the UK and to make recommendations about future developments.

The subsequent report and recommendations had massive implications for training colleges and for teacher training in general, which will be considered in Chapter 3.

Conclusion

This chapter discussed the origins and development of teacher training in the UK once education was accepted as a right for all children, not just for those of the upper classes. The history of teacher training from the nineteenth century to the Second World War is briefly discussed, as are the various models of training employed. These include monitoring, apprenticeship and theoretically based methods. The origins of training colleges, the beginnings of university involvement and initial attempts at research into teacher training complete the first part of the chapter.

The second part of the chapter examines the rapid expansion of teacher training after 1944 and is set in the context of the times – particularly in relation to the McNair Report, the 1944 Education Act and the ETS.

The role of government and the local authorities after the war is considered as a large number of new training colleges opened. The implications of the Crowther Report in 1959 are set out and the following years, which led up to the Robbins Report in 1962, are examined.

3

THE CONSENSUS IN EDUCATION BEGINS TO UNRAVEL

Introduction

At the end of Chapter 2, we introduced the Robbins Report of 1963 (DES, 1963b), the result of the work of a committee set up to consider the future of higher education (HE) in England and Wales. The first section of this chapter begins by discussing the report in detail and considers its implications for teacher training. As in Chapter 2, some of the implications are given substance by reference to three particular colleges, which show something of the range of institutions affected. The Robbins Report was followed by three government-sponsored papers which are discussed here in terms of how they relate to teacher training – the Newsom Report (DES, 1963a), the Plowden Report (DES, 1967) and Circular 10/65 (DES, 1965).

This chapter demonstrates that the period up to 1970 was notable for the consensus between the political parties with regard to education. Government was only involved in funding and deciding the large organisational issues with regard to schools, colleges and universities. What went on within schools and within HE was the business of teachers and lecturers. The national press tended to take a similar 'neutral' position. At the end of the 1960s, however, this 'consensus' started to unravel – a process that became more evident after the general election of 1970.

As the economic position deteriorated and 'the permissive society' began to attract the attention of conservative politicians and the press, teachers and teacher trainers were seen to be undermining the traditional establishment and the economic wellbeing of the country. This concern developed into significant criticism and was partly responsible for the setting up of the James Committee in 1972. The committee's report included reference to teacher training and the second half of this chapter considers the detail of the James Report and its outcomes, in the context of teacher training. It also looks at the basis and outcomes of the 'attacks' on the educational practices made at the time, how they continued throughout the 1970s and started what became known as 'the Great Debate'.

The James Report was followed by a government white paper – 'A Framework for Expansion' (DES, 1972a), a green paper (DES, 1977) and an HMI survey (DES, 1979), all of which had significant implications for teacher training.

1962–70

Since the end of the Second World War in 1945, the country had struggled with aspects of the post-war recovery. There was rationing of food and much housing and infrastructure required rebuilding. By the 1960s, however, things were improving and the economy had started to grow. One of the major concerns was the perception of inequality in educational provision (McKenzie, 2001). Partly as a result of this, the Robbins Report, which dealt with HE in general (but included substantial reference to teacher training), was followed by reports and government papers which were aimed at educational provision in schools. 'Half Our Future' Newsom (DES, 1963a), 'Circular 10/65' (DES, 1965) and 'Children and Their Primary Schools' Plowden (DES, 1967) are examples of this process and they all had significant implications for teacher training. Newsom dealt with the education of children with less than average ability, Circular 10/65 with possible formats of secondary education and Plowden with primary education.

Para 300 of the Newsom Report specifically asked ministers to ensure that their views were passed to the Robbins committee which was working at the same time. These reports and Circular 10/65 will be discussed below after considering the Robbins Report.

The Robbins Report and its implications

The report contained two chapters devoted to teacher training and dealt with the subject in the context of HE in general. The thrust of the overall report was towards expansion of the whole HE sector. The report began by noting that institutions of HE in Great Britain (including colleges of education for teacher training) could not be described as part of a system, since they had grown up independently. The report noted that there were 146 teacher training institutions ranging in size from 1,000 to less than 500 students. The number of students in teacher training was 31,000 in 1958/9 and 49,000 in 1962. In relation to teacher training, the report makes significant reference to the McNair Report (Board of Education, 1944) and notes the urgent need to increase the number of students in teacher training. The report advocated an increase in the number of students training to be teachers to 82,000 by 1970/1. This increase was mirrored in the required increase in student numbers as a whole in HE, which it was suggested should be increased seven-fold from the level of 100,000 in the early 1950s.

The Robbins Report reflected on the need to improve the quality of teachers and the desire to make teaching an all-graduate profession. Robbins advocated that suitably qualified third-year HE students ought to have the opportunity to go on to a degree and teaching qualification. It followed this up by noting that graduates with professional training were regarded by schools as more competent and useful than those with a basic degree qualification (para 328); a point as relevant in secondary schools as in primary schools. The length of the degree course for teachers was also discussed. Robbins thought that a course for teachers definitely needed an education studies element (see Chapter 2 and below) which meant that with two specialist subjects a four-year course was inevitable. Specialist courses in, for example, physical education, domestic science, music and art and craft were also to be encouraged and maintained, particularly in colleges which were offering them at the time.

In the colleges, the implementation of these proposals raised significant issues, often particular to the individual institutions. Most colleges would struggle to cope with increased numbers. Robbins had suggested that there ought to be six new universities and that ten of the existing HE institutions become universities. Two thousand students was seen as a minimum number of students if an institution was to have university status.

The college at Worcester, which had only recently doubled in size to nearly 500 students and where building work was still in progress, began to consider the possibility of becoming a university (Cheesewright, 2008). Within the college, 'elevation' to university status by 1980 was seen as a realistic possibility, but it was anticipated that there would be competition from several nearby institutions. Colleges at Gloucester, Kidderminster, Bromsgrove, Hereford and Wolverhampton might aspire to similar status. In the event, Kidderminster, Bromsgrove and Hereford closed and Wolverhampton received university status before Worcester – which achieved this aim in 2005.

In 1963, however, the initial difficulty in Worcester was to gain support from the city council, which seemed rather reluctant to countenance a much larger student body in the city. The college also had to lobby the government to consider increasing college numbers to the suggested minimum of 2,000. Worcester was soon authorised to grow to almost 1,000 and became Worcester College of Education in 1965. Further expansion was allowed in the period up to 1969 since further teacher shortages were envisaged. Money for building extra facilities, however, was not forthcoming and hence students had to find accommodation outside the campus.

Academically there was also upheaval – Robbins advocated a four-year Bachelor of Education degree course, in which the three-year certificate was a constituent and to which a special subject would be added. The University of Birmingham, with whom Worcester was associated, wanted the choice of extra courses to be subjects which were taught at Birmingham. This removed the possibility of students specialising in those subjects which were the traditional strengths of Worcester – rural studies, domestic science and some aspects of physical education. In addition, it was felt that Birmingham was being rather too rigid in the way it dictated to associated colleges and expected to have all fourth-year students taught in Birmingham. Following a path taken by other institutions, the decision was taken to validate the degrees from Worcester via the Council for National Academic Awards (CNAA), which would raise no problems associated with subject specialisms. CNAA had to approve the syllabuses and oversee the examinations. It was seen as a move towards independence in the process of achieving university status.

St Mary's College in Cheltenham was similarly influenced by the Robbins Report, despite being in the throes of earlier expansion and building programmes. It was decided to concentrate on alleviating the shortage of primary teachers by concentrating on the training of women teachers. In 1964 the college was associated with the School of Education of the University of Bristol, which awarded their Bachelor of Education degrees. As at Worcester, the expanded course would be in two stages, with the certificate course being supplemented by a theory of education course, plus an extra year of further study in the main subject (Challinor, 1978). However, the numbers of the first cohort who chose to continue from the certificate to the fourth year were small. The course began in 1965 with specialist facilities shared with St Paul's College, a training college for men which was situated nearby in the town.

Coventry College of Education was also affected by the Robbins Report and, although the circumstances were rather different, the issues were the same as at Worcester. Canley College had become Coventry College of Education in 1964 and whereas in 1960 there had been just over 400 students, by the end of the decade there were almost 1,400. The certificate course had been expanded to a three-year course in 1960 and just as at Cheltenham in 1965 the first students entered with an opportunity to study a four-year degree course. The problem associated with the four-year degree was that the University of Birmingham, with which it was associated, would not accept the proposals for an honours degree, or for the development of a degree course which included physical education or practical subjects like art and craft – essential for aspiring primary schoolteachers. Consequently, negotiations took place with the aim of linking with the new University of Warwick, which began to award the degrees in 1969. Coventry College of Education also started a one-year PGCE course for postgraduate students in a variety of subjects – predominately aimed at aspiring secondary schoolteachers (Abbott, 2008).

These developments clearly led to a significant increase in numbers. There were initiatives to increase awareness of the use of educational technology in schools and link closely with the nearby inner-city schools of Coventry. Programmes to train teachers of immigrants and special needs children were advocated, all of which led to resource issues in accommodation, teaching facilities and staffing. There was a need for science laboratories and library facilities, but also for staff who were suitably qualified to teach to degree level, and who were also familiar with schoolteaching practice.

At no point did the government of any political party attempt to influence the curriculum or the way aspiring teachers were trained to teach. In this respect they adhered to the tenets laid down by the McNair Report (Board of Education, 1944) of the war years, which were followed throughout the period of 'consensus' in education (Abbott et al., 2013). Issues to do with the school organisation, the curriculum content in schools and styles of teaching were left to 'the professionals'.

The government dealt only with issues such as a shortage of teachers, a perceived lack of quality of the teaching force and gross inequalities in education provision. These were met in varying degrees by measures to increase numbers in teacher training and improve the facilities in both colleges and universities – measures which inevitably had to be paid for out of the public purse.

Half Our Future

The Newsom Report (DES, 1963a) was an attempt to begin the study of inequality in the secondary school system. Published a week before Robbins, pupils of average and less than average ability in secondary education were studied.

Recommendations were made to improve the situation of such pupils in secondary modern schools. The chair, John Newsome, had experience as the chief education officer of Hertfordshire and his team included Alec Clegg, chief education officer of the West Riding of Yorkshire, and other serving schoolteachers.

Average and below-average children made up three quarters of the secondary school population, but pro rata were allocated significantly less resources than those children who attended grammar schools and were following an academic curriculum. In various parts of industrial cities and elsewhere, poor housing and social conditions resulted in children from poor backgrounds often also receiving an unsatisfactory education. In particular, the school buildings were deficient and the teaching staff disillusioned. Some staff remained in a school for one term only and they were often newly trained teachers. In many secondary modern schools, subjects were taught by teachers who were unqualified in those subjects. Thus in many schools, form teachers were expected to teach English, maths and religious education to their own class, regardless of their own qualifications (paras 283–4). In addition, the youngest and least experienced staff were frequently allocated to teach the most difficult classes.

Newsom made many recommendations that had direct or indirect implications for teacher training:

1. Research was needed into teaching techniques for pupils who had deprived environmental and linguistic backgrounds. In this context, it was further noted that in the Crowther Report, para 277 (see Chapter 2), it had been suggested that teachers' conditions of service and pay scales ought to recognise the challenges of teaching in difficult schools. Nothing had been done to implement this recommendation.
2. The practice of grouping pupils by ability needed to be reduced.
3. Pupils ought to be introduced to a wider range of subjects including the arts.
4. The final year in school ought to introduce students to the adult world.

However, beyond these issues the Newsom Report also included a significant section (chapter 12) specifically directed at teacher training, both in colleges and university schools of education. It was felt that there must be training which ensured that teachers had an opportunity to enhance their own subject knowledge and also their pedagogical knowledge. Students needed a specialist subject and at least one subsidiary subject and they needed to be prepared to teach older pupils once the school leaving age was raised. They also needed preparing for the challenges arising from teaching pupils from deprived linguistic, social and environmental backgrounds.

In addition, teachers needed to understand the implications of research into education and aspects of sociology, social history and child development, particularly as related to adolescence. There were links to be made with the training of social workers, youth leaders and other professionals in the field. These recommendations were to apply to university- and college-trained teachers.

These and other findings of the committee led Newsom to note the implications for the Robbins Report and for HE, both in terms of children coming out of schools to study in colleges and universities and also with particular respect to the future training of teachers.

Circular 10/65

As has been previously noted, one of the main drivers of educational change in this era was the need to have more equality of educational provision. One means of doing this was seen to be the establishment of a comprehensive system of secondary education, instead of the existing grammar/secondary modern divide in which selection at age 11 was the norm. To facilitate this, the Labour government brought out Circular 10/65, requesting local education authorities (LEAs) to submit plans for the reorganisation of education in their areas. Various systems were proposed, but it was accepted that one size would not fit all. Middle schools and sixth form colleges were introduced into many authorities, even though there was little or no research into the problems or benefits to be derived from different types of school. Since the LEAs were only requested to submit plans, rather than required to comply, those who were opposed to the move were able to delay the process until a government more sympathetic to the grammar/secondary modern divide was elected in 1970. In fact the debate was still raging in 2016, with the education secretary and prime minister both advocating a return to a kind of selective education (DfE, 2016). Some LEAs had successfully refused to comply with Circular 10/65 for over 50 years.

The circular accepted that there would be implications for school building programmes, but staffing ratios, staff training and initial teacher training were not seen as particular issues. Any local authority which decided to use sixth form colleges would expect to attract plenty of specialist staff, who would want to go there precisely because of the opportunity to do high-level work. On the other hand, there was concern that some middle schools would struggle to find teachers with the expertise to teach young adolescents of high ability. In the context of the recommendations regarding specialist teachers in both the Crowther and Newsom Reports, this seemed to anticipate staffing problems, which LEAs would be required to address when deciding which scheme might be most appropriate for their area. A shortage of teachers in 1969 was anticipated, but there was no proposal to increase the numbers of teachers in training and no specific reference to initial teacher training. Schools, LEAs and teacher unions were urged to work together to help teachers cope in schools. In the event, those LEAs which 'went comprehensive' set up patterns of organisation which were extremely varied. Some middle schools had pupils of 9–13 years, others 9–12 and others 11–14 years. Some LEAs embraced comprehensive education but kept a single division at 11 years.

Teacher trainers had to determine for themselves how to cope with training teachers for so many varied systems – some simply 'extended' their primary courses to include reference to the 'middle' years, whereas others continued as before. Thus, in some colleges, courses were modified to acquaint students with the needs of a middle school age range of perhaps 9–14 years.

The Plowden Report: Children and Their Primary Schools

This report was initiated when the 11-plus ceased to be used in many LEAs. When the need to select children on academic ability at age 11 years disappeared, primary schools could become child-centred rather than exam-centred. The curriculum became more suited to individual learning and could capitalise on the interests of children. The methods of teaching could be more flexible than previously, and children enabled to progress at their own pace. These factors were helped by the changing environment in education and society at large. Gillard (2011) sees the educational context as one of increasing professionalism and expertise of teachers and of excitement, creativity and innovation in schools. The social context was the 'swinging sixties' where people were shedding the inhibitions of their parents in music, the arts and everyday life.

The report begins by noting that it starts from the premise that the child is the basis on which all teaching should be based. What is desirable for the child and what is attainable ought to be the foundation of practice within schools. There is reference to the pre-war Hadow Report (Board of Education, 1933) as the basis of the system within which the Plowden Committee was working. The premise of Hadow was that what the wise and good parent desired for their child must be what the nation desired for its children. In primary education, children ought to be given the opportunity for creativity and learning, based on the child's interests rather than on learning facts for regurgitation. Not surprisingly, the report paid a good deal of attention to what was happening in teacher training.

The practice of recruiting untrained graduates to teaching was not considered helpful in primary education and indeed the report advocates that the practice cease (para 969). Schools had criticised the use of untrained university graduates in schools and preferred to recruit from colleges of education. However, in some cases the colleges taught too much theory and too little practice. It was noted that in the main, graduates who went on to complete a PGCE usually taught in secondary schools and that efforts ought to be made to attract them to primary schools. The number of university departments in England and Wales which offered PGCE courses needed increasing in number, in order to improve the numbers of graduate teachers in primary schools. The advent of a Bachelor of Education qualification was seen as a way forward in improving the situation and moving towards an all-graduate profession. Lady Plowden echoed Newsom in wanting teacher training linked to the training provision for social and youth workers, in order to alert teachers to the backgrounds from which some of their pupils came.

Since primary teachers were normally expected to teach a whole range of subjects including mathematics, science, English and music, there was a need for recruits to be better qualified in more subjects than was the case at the time. The curriculum knowledge of students needed improvement. Courses in the colleges needed to include training in two main subjects if possible and include educational studies and substantial periods of teaching practice, some as early as possible in the course. Child psychology, sociology and philosophy ought to be included. Music, drama, physical education and the arts subjects must not be lost. Plowden realised there would be staffing problems for the colleges. For a degree-level course, lecturers were required who could teach at a high level *and* who had experience of working in primary schools. The report also noted the need to recruit men to teach in primary schools – an issue which has continued up to the present day.

In the colleges, as has been demonstrated above, some of these issues were already being tackled as a result of earlier developments, but as the 'Plowden' ideals began to permeate primary schools, there was an expectation in some schools that colleges would supply newly trained primary staff conversant in child-centred practices. Similarly, there was a need for newly trained secondary staff who were ready for the development of comprehensive education (Abbott, 2008).

However, at the end of the 1960s, funding for education was lacking, because so much money had already been spent in implementing the Robbins Report. Education was already mortgaged (Halsey and Sylva, 1987). Thus, many of the recommendations of the reports and of Circular 10/65 did not have a significant impact on the schools and hence on the practices of teachers. In practice, the reports had all concentrated on their own concerns in education. They had also put forward general recommendations about practices in schools and about teacher training. There had been a number of common concerns, such as education in deprived areas, links to parents and communities and an expansion of nursery provision. These were all areas in which teacher training had a role to play. There was a need for increased numbers of teachers in training, with higher entry qualifications and greater specialist expertise. Better salaries and ways of attracting the best teachers to the most deprived schools were pre-requisites for a future education system which would give all children the chance to reach their full potential. However, as an election approached at the end of the 1960s these would be issues, costly issues, for a new government to face.

1970–9

The end of 'consensus' impacts on teacher education

The election of 1970 had been lost by Harold Wilson's Labour Party and, although education was not a major issue in the election, all parties seemed committed to growth in the sector (Abbott et al., 2013). The Conservatives, who won the election, indicated that nursery education and primary education in poor areas would be a priority, along with raising the school leaving age. Nevertheless, resourcing such an expansion was going to be problematic. Taylor (2008) noted that it was during this period, around the election, that it became clear that teachers and teacher education had become a focus of attention for politicians, the media, the business community and the public at large. The time in which teachers and their practices were dictated by their own professionalism disappeared, as they became blamed for many of the ills in society. The primary reason for this attention was economic, as the country faced high unemployment and rising inflation. Education was coming to be seen as a tool to improve economic growth and prosperity, rather than as an end in itself.

Discussion about the purpose and nature of education in a competitive economic climate became more intense (Abbott et al., 2013). Teacher training was inevitably a part of the educational establishment that was questioned, especially as the party now in power saw some teachers as left-wing agitators who were intent upon indoctrinating children into their own ideology – a view that would lead to the ideas expressed by Kenneth Baker, a later minister of education (Abbott et al., 2013).

A series of Black Papers, written by critics of education policy, were taking issue with so-called 'libertarian values', which were seen to originate from egalitarian policies fermented in teacher training and in schools and transmitted by teachers to their students, see for example Cox and Dyson (1969). Lawson and Silva (1973) suggested that, of the many problems seen to be facing the country in the 1970s, teachers and teacher trainers were seen as one of the most intransigent. They needed to be controlled (Abbott et al., 2013) and that was one of the reasons why the new government set up the James Committee in 1972, to investigate teacher training – the first major attempt to do so since the Second World War.

To the Conservative government elected in 1970, the needs of the education system were expensive and thus implementation of recommendations was slow. As has been noted, the decision about comprehensive education had previously been left to individual LEAs to decide and although the Labour government had been supportive of the policy, the Conservative government which regained power in 1970 was considerably less favourable to a system that undermined selective education. While Ted Heath, the Conservative prime minister, committed Margaret Thatcher, his minister of education, to continue the policy, she was more in sympathy with those who wished to keep grammar schools (Abbott et al., 2013). Disquiet with comprehensive ideals can be seen as one of the first signs that education was about to become a party political 'football'.

Another sign, as McKenzie (2001) noted, was the response to parts of the Plowden Report (1967), which had generated an inordinate amount of controversy in a hostile press and among some members of Parliament. The controversy was one into which teacher trainers were inevitably drawn. Criticism of Plowden focussed on the supposed link between child-centred teaching methods and the 'permissive' society of the 1960s. Although the report is still discussed half a century later, it did not seem to have had a great impact in schools at the time. For example, the 'Three Wise Men' report of 1992 (Alexander et al., 1992) pointed out that there was very little evidence that 'progressive' methods had taken root in primary schools.

In the decade which followed Plowden, Bennett (1976) carried out research that was represented in the media as showing that 'progressive' methods were not working. Many criticised these representations, but there can be little doubt that Plowden generated more political response than pedagogical change. More work by Bennett ten years later (Bennett 1987) noted that teachers were certainly having difficulty making decisions about teaching styles and curriculum development when their specialist curriculum expertise was inadequate. Some of the main psychological theories used in the Plowden Report were easily misunderstood and too complex to be applied easily in classroom situations. Thus there was little evidence of them having made a significant impact on teaching practice.

Another aspect of the growing divide between the main political parties was any suggestion of positive discrimination to assist the situation in deprived areas, as suggested in the reports outlined above. Conservative governments were ideologically less concerned with considering problems caused by inequality and generally more concerned to maintain selection in schools. The reports cited above had strongly advocated methods to attract experienced teachers to teach children of average and below-average ability and to work in deprived areas, to increase the provision of nursery education and to link teacher training to the training of youth workers and social workers.

With this in mind, education priority areas (EPAs) were set up by the Labour secretary of state, Anthony Crosland, but only just prior to the election in 1970 which Labour lost. They were part of a positive discrimination programme of the type advocated in the Plowden Report (Abbott et al., 2013). Home/school links were encouraged and in this context much attention given to the role of language, in the learning of children whose language was seen to be restricting their cognitive development. The EPA project advisor A.H. Halsey argued for changes in teacher training to take account of these developments (Halsey and Sylva, 1987) and in many colleges, these factors did become part of the curriculum of students. However, under the Conservative government, the EPA programme inevitably lost momentum. As well as Conservative politicians there were other critics of such 'compensatory education' programmes. Bernstein (1970), for example, argued that education was not able to make up for the shortcomings in society at large, which helped create the disparity of achievement between children from different backgrounds. In the end, the scale of the EPA project was restricted and where

Plowden had argued that 300 schools were in need of special status, the project was limited to 130 schools. Largely through lack of political will, the whole EPA project came to an end in 1974.

Although salaries were enhanced to encourage teachers to apply for posts in areas of particular need, the increments were marginal (McKenzie, 2001). Kogan (1987) suggested that one of the implications of the above reports, and a possible reason why they failed to bring about significant change in practice, was that teachers were expected to become agents of social change. He considered that many teachers, and by implication their trainers, did not see themselves as such – it was simply not part of their job.

Winkley (1987) suggested that teachers needed to review their own prejudices and practice in order to deliver what children required and what the local community expected. In addition, he noted that although some schools had developed community links over a period of time and were comfortable with parents routinely coming into schools, the government and many LEAs had not responded to the needs of inner-city schools and their communities.

For teacher education, the means by which these issues of community involvement, ethnicity, compensatory education, 'progressive methods' and styles of teaching was left to individual institutions. There was no curriculum for teacher training which was laid down by an overarching national body, although as we have argued, some primary schools were wanting teachers capable of implementing new practices in education and many secondary schools needed help in developing comprehensive education. Most colleges included such training under the general title of education studies, which was soon to become a target of the criticism levelled at teacher training institutions, particularly by right-leaning commentators – criticism that can be traced back to nineteenth-century debates about the nature of teacher training.

Education studies

Education Studies was a common factor in courses during this decade as they expanded to three- and four-year programmes. The general term 'education studies' encompassed a wide range of studies which included varying amounts of sociology, psychology, history of education and the philosophy of education. These were generally linked closely to the work done in schools and referred to as 'the Four Disciplines of Education'. Although at the time education studies arose as a result of suggestions from the reports listed above, and were generally accepted as valuable parts of the teacher training curriculum, they would come to be seen by some as the root of what was later perceived to be a fundamental flaw in the training of teachers.

Woods (1972) set out the predominant academic view at the time – that this work was essential in any teacher training programme. Teachers have to take account of the sociological aspects of the environments in which their pupils are being brought up. Philosophy is required to make decisions about the curriculum to be taught and psychology is essential to the teacher when thinking of a child's intelligence and motivation. The arguments for and against selection in secondary education and the age of transfer need careful analytical thinking in relation to their previous and ongoing impact on the local and national community. Thus, a knowledge of the history of education is important to place policy developments in context. Woods (1972) also set out some guidelines about possible ways to include these studies in undergraduate and post-graduate programmes. In post-graduate programmes, it was assumed that graduates would have sufficient academic subject knowledge to teach their subject and thus a PGCE year could be spent concentrating on education studies, which included the four disciplines and aspects of how to teach their main subjects. Practice of teaching was to be gained in the first or probationary year of teaching in school. Students in training colleges could study the four disciplines throughout the undergraduate programme and might move into the probationary year after completing the degree. For qualified teachers who had not studied these 'essential' disciplines, Woods advocated in-service training programmes to enable serving teachers to gain the necessary expertise.

Woods (1972) remarked that teachers and other professionals in schools needed to beware of the pressure from ideological, economic, political and social groups trying to make schools conform to their own agenda. Understanding the values of these groups and how they sought to influence educational practice was essential for teachers, who must not be indoctrinated or seek to indoctrinate their students. Perhaps this was the aspect which most irritated the critics of education studies and who broadly felt that politicians not academics ought to take charge of what was being taught to trainee teachers. Lawlor (1990), one of the most strident critics of education studies, wrote about the malaise that she felt had overtaken education and the training of teachers in the 1970s, before the reforms of teacher education in the 1980s. Lawlor claims that the problems with teacher education began with the proliferation of departments and faculties of education which taught education studies including sociology. She advocated the removal of some aspects of theory from the training of teachers and suggested that teachers needed more practice in schools in order to become competent professionals. Aspects of multiculturalism and language across the curriculum in an English course at one university were singled out for particular criticism by Lawlor. Indeed, several university PGCE courses were used as examples of the way that, in her view, education studies had influenced young teachers and led to 'progressive theories' infiltrating the work of teachers.

This lack of attention to the content of the subject seems to be justified when she cites a lack of knowledge of the second or subsidiary subject that many students were studying. For teachers of children of higher ability, who were aiming to take advanced-level exams in some secondary schools, knowledge of the subject to advanced level by the teacher was probably not sufficient. Yet for many PGCE courses it was deemed acceptable. Lawlor points to the same perceived problems in Bachelor of Education courses for both primary and secondary teachers. She felt that teaching practice on these courses was undermined by professional studies and education studies and again cites various courses in detail.

development in schools and, by implication, to knowledge which informed teacher training. The Schools Council was an organisation set up ten years earlier to promote curriculum development and teaching methods in schools. According to Lowe (1997), the work of this organisation was very significant in the age of 'teacher autonomy'. It was later abolished when the Conservative government of the late 1970s disagreed with its work in promoting educational innovation (Abbott et al., 2013).

The James Report was one of the first documents to refer to the principles and methods of educational technology as an important factor in the knowledge that teachers needed in their work. It noted how the existing structure of courses was causing problems in colleges, as the tutors tried to extend the student's level of HE and complete their professional training. It was difficult to recruit tutors who had a sufficiently high level of academic expertise, combined with suitable experience in schools – particularly at the primary level. Courses often lacked balance, as institutions tried to do too many things at once and produce the 'finished article', i.e. a fully competent teacher, after a single period of training on a PGCE or Bachelor of Education course. The following probationary year was particularly problematic for schools and colleges.

In notes about the perceived background to the report, it was observed that the existing training was not always a suitable preparation for teachers taking on the new roles and responsibilities that were becoming evident in the reorganised school system. The advent of first, middle and comprehensive schools, the raising of the school leaving age and the small but necessary extension of nursery education were bringing new challenges to schools and teachers. Considering that the shortage of teachers was supposedly coming to an end, the report goes on to propose some radical changes to teacher training which, it suggested, be divided into three cycles. In addition, a revision of the qualification process was proposed. It further suggested that provision ought to be made for students who intended to teach to study alongside those training for other professions.

The three cycles of training

These were explained by James in reverse order, because the third part was to be seen as vital if any of the recommendations were to be accepted. Training in an institution would last approximately three years. The first cycle was to do with what James refers to as 'personal education'. The second was pre-service training and induction when those students specifically wanting to enter the teaching profession would begin their professional training. The third was in-service education and training.

Cycle 1: personal education

There was an assumption that recruits to Cycle 2 – the professional training – would have achieved a good standard of HE in their Cycle 1 studies in colleges and universities. The initial cycle (of perhaps two years' duration) might include some aspects of the study of education, in terms of theoretical and practical expertise. A hope was expressed that the institutions would enable this to happen within a general HE programme. The work would aim for a Diploma in Higher Education, which would include degree-level work and open up the possibility of a joint degree. There ought to be a wide range of choice, since some participants would go on to work with young people in another capacity such as social workers or youth workers. It would be desirable to include aspects of philosophy, sociology, history of education and psychology.

Cycle 2

Professional training for teachers would begin at this point and be in two phases over two years. The first phase would be spent in an institution, with the study specifically aimed at students expecting to go into school in the following year. The second phase would be spent teaching in a school or further education college and regarded as the first post of the teacher as a probationer, with a salary paid in the normal way.

Cycle 3

This stage in the training was envisaged as being the most important by the committee, since it was generally accepted that initial teacher training was not sufficient in itself to equip teachers for the variety and constantly changing demands of the school system. To cope with the demands of a modern society and of pupils of differing ages, ethnicities and mother tongues, teachers must be enabled to: 'extend their personal education, develop their professional competence and improve their understanding of educational principles and techniques' (para 2.2).

Thus Cycle 3 advocated a comprehensive in-service training programme, which would provide serving teachers with a much needed opportunity to develop and improve practice. The programmes available would be broad in scope and range from weekend or evening courses and conferences to long-term secondments, study for degrees and higher degrees. There would be release for curriculum development meetings, and opportunities to engage in research and educational projects.

The committee noted that although the Department for Education and Skills, LEAs, HMI, universities, colleges and the Schools Council already provided some opportunities, there was a lack of planning and coordination which meant that in-service training was piecemeal. The existing provision was also seen to be poorly funded and to cover only a fraction of what was necessary. The relevant bodies and the teachers were encouraged to work together. An important point was made, that although the future requirements of the profession could not be anticipated, satisfactory in-service provision must be based upon a clear idea of the needs to be met. These included a deepened knowledge of teaching method, educational theory, educational technology, educational research and experiment.

It was anticipated that teachers in primary schools would be particularly in need of knowledge of language development, the teaching of reading and writing, an expansion of subject knowledge and the introduction of French into the primary curriculum. Secondary teachers were expected to require increased expertise in their second subjects, special needs training, shortage subject development and insights into working in multicultural classrooms.

Beyond these aspects of training, the new programmes ought to give the opportunity for the retraining of teachers who wished to return to teaching after a break and for aspiring heads, deputy heads and other school managers to understand management techniques.

Implementation

The report does not ignore the problems of putting such a three-cycle programme into operation. For schools and further education colleges, the implications were mainly that there would be an obligation to teachers to enable the training within their organisational structures. This would go far beyond the 'laissez faire' attitude which existed in some schools towards new teachers and in-service training. For universities and colleges the implications were much wider. The report advocated the setting up of professional centres where expertise would be provided by LEA advisers, experienced teachers and tutors who maintained close links with schools and were up to date in their knowledge of curriculum development and educational research. These centres might be developed from existing teacher centres or operate from colleges or other institutions of HE. They would need to gain recognition and satisfy standards, so that there was continuity across the sector.

The financial implications were also considered, with finance coming from LEAs and the area training organisations. These latter were seen as outdated. They had arisen from recommendations of the McNair Committee (see Chapter 2), but after the Robbins Report (DES, 1963b) and nearly 30 years of existence, the James Committee recommended they be superseded by regional organisations, which would have other educational functions beyond professional training (para 5.22).

The committee was against (though not unanimously) the retention of the existing system of teacher training, which they felt was too strongly influenced by the demands of the universities. 'The effect of university control can, at its worst, be one of enervation' (para 5.17). Colleges, through their area training organisations, had links with institutes or schools of education within universities, but the function of the institutes and schools in universities was only dimly understood by those with overall power within those institutions. This meant that teaching qualifications and training were of only marginal concern to the senates of universities. A much better option, in the opinion of a majority, would be the setting up of regional authorities and professional centres and to bring all participants in training together. The proposed Diploma in Higher Education (see Cycle 1), via CNAA, could be used to give credibility to the qualifications for teachers.

Reaction to the report

This plan for teacher training might have sounded like a utopian vision from the point of view of some teachers and aspiring teachers, but the teaching unions and the government took a different view. The report came out at a time of financial hardship in the country, and a falling birth rate meant that there was seen to be a distinct surplus of teachers. Consequently, in addition to the James Report, a white paper, 'A Framework for Expansion' (DES, 1972a), and a government paper, 'Circular 7/73' (DES, 1973), followed from the Department for Education. These documents suggested that teachers who had successfully completed probation were to be called 'registered teachers'. Some provisions within James were to be instigated with regard to in-service training.

An all-graduate profession was still to be the target, with continued support for the three- and four-year Bachelor of Education courses. The courses would contain education studies and teaching practice, which would extend to 15 weeks. The Diploma in Higher Education was accepted, as was the CNAA process of validation. Regional councils were to take the place of the area training organisations and there was to be an Advisory Council on the Training and Supply of Teachers. The number of student teachers was to be halved, but the number gaining their qualifications via the PGCE was to be increased. The financing of any changes to teacher education was left for LEAs and education committees to bear.

In the event, colleges did diversify their courses to attract students who were not aiming to be teachers. Some colleges and institutions of HE amalgamated (e.g. Crewe with Alsager, Northampton College of Arts and the College of Education in Corby); some closed (e.g. Bromsgrove and Kidderminster). There were efforts to increase the involvement of colleges and departments of education in in-service education (Nowotny, 1977). CNAA became seen as a validating body, enabling the involvement of a wider range of staff in creating awards, which recognised the need for greater flexibility in the award programmes.

For example, the initial teacher training programme at Coventry College of Education was expanded, both in terms of the number of PGCE programmes and the development of the Bachelor of Education course. The scope of the in-service programmes was expanded and even included one-year full-time secondment opportunities. In addition, serious discussions began about either becoming part of a local college of technology or of nearby Warwick University. At St Mary's in Cheltenham, the Diploma of Higher Education was introduced and a wide range of non-teacher education courses included in the prospectus. There was significantly more liaison with two other local institutions of HE, with whom plans were made to set up new PGCE and Bachelor of Education courses validated by CNAA. Worcester College followed a similar path, with CNAA validating degrees from 1976. The college was divided into three academic schools, arts, sciences and teaching studies, in order to attract students who would make up the numbers lost by the cut in student teachers.

It is clear that the reports and papers of this period could have contributed to a major transformation and coordinated the reorganisation of teacher education. In the event, implementation of the recommendations was largely piecemeal.

The Great Debate

As was seen above, the James Report was instigated partly in response to a somewhat frenzied media campaign, to have the roles of teachers and teacher trainers clarified with the aim of reverting to a more traditional style of education. The attacks on the educational establishment continued in a series of broadly right-wing pamphlets – the Black Papers (Cox and Dyson, 1969). They were published throughout the 1970s and were focussed on progressive educational practices and egalitarian trends supposedly being encouraged in schools and colleges.

In 1976, they were supplemented by the then prime minister James Callaghan in a speech at Ruskin College Oxford, which was seen to start off a 'Great Debate'. Fundamentally, the debate was about how education could best be made to serve the needs of a capitalist economy and was used by those on the right to attack what they called progressive educational policies.

Shirley Williams, the new secretary of state for education, presented a green paper (DES, 1977) as a contribution to the debate, but also as a continuation of 'A Framework for Expansion' (DES, 1972a). Many points in the green paper had implications for teacher training and later Williams reflected that it had been a precursor to the sweeping changes instigated by a later Conservative government (Abbott et al., 2013). The green paper began by making some of the same points as previous reports and rehearsing some issues which indicated how little had changed in some respects during previous years. There was still a high turnover of teachers, particularly in geographical locations where the children needed the help of experienced teachers who would remain in the school for several years. Teachers were finding difficulty in changing their styles of teaching to suit the new demands of the changing organisational patterns in schools.

Encouragingly, however, there was no evidence (in spite of the impression given in some quarters) of a decline in educational standards. Nevertheless, it was suggested that regional conferences take place involving schools, LEAs and training institutions, parents, business interests, churches, the Schools Council and trade unions. They would consider the curriculum, assessment, teacher training and the school-to-work transition, where education professionals were seen to have little experience.

The regional conferences which occurred were seen later by Shirley Williams as having been useful ways of bringing people together and coordinating approaches to best practice (Abbott et al., 2013). With regard to teacher training, the green paper noted the number of two-year-trained teachers still serving, in an environment which was moving towards an all-graduate profession. Inevitably, these teachers would be less conversant with up-to-date ideas about teaching and the management of schools and it was perceived that there was a significant need for in-service work with this group.

Entry qualifications for teaching training were seen as in need of strengthening – particularly with regard to English and maths. The size and content of the teacher training curriculum was seen to have changed due to the introduction of the Bachelor of Education courses, though it was accepted that due to financial restraints, these courses were largely three years rather than four years in length. The aim to have an all-graduate profession was now expected to be achievable by 1979/80. With this in particular, the reformed Advisory Committee for the Supply and Training of Teachers was supportive (Becher, 1992).

Colleges would be expected to become centres of professional expertise as advocated by the James Committee and work on all aspects of teacher training. Newly qualified teachers would be entitled to one day a week of extra training and serving teachers were to help in developing skills in English, mathematics, multicultural education and management skills. Much was also expected of LEAs and schools in facilitating the work.

There were inevitable financial restraints which would inhibit spending, but the green paper emphasised that because of the falling birth rate there ought to be more flexibility in the system than had been the case previously. The secretary of state would continue to be advised by the Advisory Council for the Training and Supply of Teachers about the numbers of trainees needed in future. Williams said later that it had provoked a valuable debate, which continued right up to 1979 when a series of HMI reports and surveys had implications for teacher training (Abbott et al., 2013).

One survey (DES, 1979) centred upon the development of the Bachelor of Education degree, which led to an ordinary degree over three years and an honours degree if a fourth year was undertaken. The survey which was started in 1976 came out in 1979, when the Bachelor of Education in colleges had only really been running for three years. It attempted to ascertain whether the degree was meeting the needs of teachers and schools. The degree programmes were found to be satisfactory, though lacking somewhat in coherence, particularly between the academic and professional parts of the courses. Personal tutors were advised to attempt to ensure continuity in the experiences of individual students. Improvement was needed in relation to special needs teaching and in introducing students to the problems of teaching classes of mixed ability and mixed ages. In primary courses, the English and maths programmes were satisfactory but some secondary teachers were not made aware of the contribution of language to all disciplines.

Following the recommendations of the earlier reports and the white paper (DES, 1972a), there was a need to coordinate the approaches to in-service training, the induction of newly qualified teachers and initial teacher training. The experience of teachers working with children from multicultural backgrounds gave cause for concern, as did the students' lack of depth in knowledge of some second subjects. Students generally needed more time on teaching practice and colleges needed better links with schools. It was suggested that teachers and lecturers spend some time doing each other's jobs. Considering how soon this survey took place after the start of the Bachelor of Education programmes, the findings were quite encouraging for colleges.

However, in 1979, the government changed and a long period of Conservative government began. The debate on the roles of teachers and their training was initially superseded by upheavals in economic and social policy, but soon the debate would become a major preoccupation of the new government.

Conclusion

This chapter has traced the development of teacher education between 1962 and 1979. It shows how comprehensive reports into HE and teacher training and a series of other government-sponsored reports and circulars made significant recommendations about education in schools and about teacher training. Some of these recommendations were implemented, but financial and political constraints precluded wholesale change.

The chapter also examined the process by which education moved in this period from being largely the province of professionals, to being the subject of political argument and polemic. The implications of this change for teacher education are discussed and developed in Chapter 4.

4

TEACHER EDUCATION AS A COMPETITIVE MARKET

Introduction

The transformation of teacher training during the period 1979–2010 is considered in two sections which correspond with the change of political party in power. However, there was little apparent change in education policy. In many respects the Labour party, which gained power in 1997, followed the lead of the previous Conservative administration. The whole period 1979–2010 saw an increase in government control of the training of teachers, through the setting up of a number of agencies and the imposition of specific standards to be monitored by Ofsted. At the same time, a variety of new modes of entry to teaching were introduced and the emphasis in training moved towards 'hands-on' practice in schools and away from academic and theoretical considerations. Government policies centred around the enabling of a 'free market' and 'competition' in all areas of public services. Education came to be seen as a tool to enable national economic growth rather than an as entitlement of all children.

A Conservative government had been elected in 1979. For the first two years of government their priority was the 'economy', following monetary policies formulated when in opposition by Margaret Thatcher, the prime minister, and Keith Joseph, one of her ministers (Abbott et al., 2013). Education policy was initially allowed to continue much as it had during the previous administration, when James Callaghan had been prime minister and Shirley Williams was in charge of education. After two years in government, in 1981 Thatcher appointed Keith Joseph as secretary of state for education and science, specifically to bring market-orientated philosophies to education. These led to radical changes in teacher training.

When a Labour government under Tony Blair was elected in 1997, education was made a priority, but although increased funding was made available, the main policy trends, including those related to teacher training, were not noticeably changed. As a result, over the complete 30-year period, the role of higher education (HE) in teacher training became significantly less important and the role of schools and 'outside agencies' correspondingly more important. The introduction and development of these ideas profoundly influenced teacher education at the time and continue to do so.

1979–97

Confronting the educational establishment

Margaret Thatcher initially appointed Mark Carlisle to be in charge of education when she took over as prime minister, leading the new government in 1979. However, she was not entirely happy with the policies he followed (Abbott et al., 2013). Keith Joseph took over from him and, although he was very much against the state system, he was enthusiastic to try to change it by confronting what he considered to be a complacent educational establishment (Ribbins and Sherratt, 1997). In this he had the strong backing of the prime minister, who had experience as education secretary in the department from 1970 to 1974. The education establishment to be confronted included local education authorities (LEAs), the teaching profession and teacher training organisations (Baker, 1993).

In relation to the latter, confrontation occurred in a number of ways which reflected the government's economic strategy and the desire to take control of the organisation, structure and curriculum content of teacher training. It took place against a background of a shortfall in teacher numbers and recruitment.

Teacher recruitment

Manpower planning was not seen as a necessary aspect of a 'free-market' philosophy (Becher, 1992). Until 1980, planning with regard to teacher numbers and allocation of training places had enabled the Advisory Committee for the Supply and Training of Teachers (ACSTT) to consider the future needs of schools and colleges and allow training institutions to recruit according to that need. Government funding followed recruitment. There had been a partnership between the DES and LEAs which meant that teacher shortages ought to have been avoided and that students entering training could have some confidence in finding employment in the profession.

In 1980, the ACSTT committee was replaced by an Advisory Committee for the Supply and Education of Teachers (ACSET), which was set up as a government quango and fell into the pattern of the new government in seeking to marginalise LEAs (Abbott et al., 2013). Prediction of teacher numbers became much less rigorous, in line with a market philosophy. Where shortages were seen to exist, bursaries were offered to students as incentives to tempt prospective teachers to teach particular subjects. The employment prospects for newly qualified teachers became uncertain and consequently recruitment fell away.

The implications of this decision were still being felt 30 years later, when Estelle Morris, one-time education secretary, pointed out that the severe shortage of teachers being felt in 2015 was the direct result of that decision (Morris, 2015). One distinguished chief education officer, Professor Tim Brighouse, remarked when interviewed for this book in 2014 that leaving the market to determine the number of students in teacher training was 'barmy'.

The Council for the Accreditation of Teacher Education

When surveys by HMI indicated that some newly qualified teachers had uncertain subject knowledge in the subjects they taught, ACSET suggested that there ought to be published guidelines on the content of teacher training. All courses should have designated minimum times, which ought to be devoted to important aspects of the teaching programmes. Ideas for further improving teacher education were developed in 'Teaching Quality' (DES, 1983), 'Circular 3/84' (DES, 1984) and a white paper, 'Better Schools' (DES, 1985). For example, with regard to subject studies it was considered necessary for primary schools to have subject specialists, who would act as consultants in the schools, possibly teaching their special subjects to classes other than their own. Schools had a majority of teachers whose expertise was in aesthetics and humanities, to the exclusion of scientific/technical subjects. Thus there was an intention to give bursaries to encourage serving teachers to do extra training in 'shortage' subjects and to encourage more applications from students who would become subject specialists in mathematics, science and technical subjects.

Although there had been minimal consultation with training organisations, ACSET went further, in proposing the setting of standards for initial teacher training (ITT) courses and for the inspection and review of provision before the approval and accreditation of courses. A body to do this – the Council for the Accreditation of Teacher Education (CATE) – was set up in 1984. CATE was expected to complete the first review of ITT within a period of three or four years.

Undoubtedly, there had been a huge diversity of provision within existing ITT courses, but now criteria existed by which all training courses were to be judged. The CATE criteria were set out in four sections – links between institutions and schools; subject studies and subject method; education and professional studies; and selection and admission.

As a result of the CATE criteria:

- PGCE courses, which had generally been of 30 weeks in length, were required to last for 36 weeks and in primary courses 200 hours had to be spent on the study of English language, and half as much time on mathematics.
- There had to be some reference to the world of economics in which the children would be growing up, and it was seen as desirable that prospective teachers should have experience of employment other than schoolteaching (DES, 1985, para 141).
- Bachelor of Education courses were required to have adequate time devoted to teaching method and subject studies.

- Students had to spend more time in schools on teaching practice and the recruitment of students had to be improved.
- Training institutions had to become more collaborative, by making formal partnership provision with schools and making sure that funds were provided to schools to pay for their increased role in training.
- Teachers would be expected to take on a proportion of the role previously fulfilled by tutors.
- Institutions needed to ensure that their own staff had recent and relevant successful experience in the classroom.

No courses were to be approved unless a local committee consisting of teachers, local business people and members of the public had scrutinised them. Information was to be collected and analysed by HMI and, although there were to be occasional visits to institutions by members of the central CATE committee, the local committees had a significant role to play in the approval of courses in their area. The overall aim was clearly to make training more practically based and to begin to move the responsibility for training onto schools.

Not surprisingly there was opposition to CATE from within teacher training institutions (Browne and Reid, 2012). Collaboration between schools and institutions had always been essential in supporting students and different models had existed within different schools – even when working with the same institution. The same varied patterns continued after the advent of CATE in 1984, although there was more formal 'training' of schoolteaching staff to undertake their 'new' roles. This training was predominantly offered to schools by their HE partners. Some schools welcomed the opportunity to have a more significant role in training and to gain some income for their efforts, other schools were more circumspect, particularly since, as part of the new regime, Ofsted were going to inspect the school provision at the same time as they inspected the institution to which the student belonged.

These innovations brought funding problems to HE providers. Not only had institutions to cope with demands from schools for money, but they had to fund the loss of their own staff, who were absent gaining recent and relevant experience in the classroom. As a consequence this led to the appointment, on short-term secondment, of serving teachers and also made it a requirement of college staff to use their preparation and non-teaching time to work in schools.

Problems also arose when students were in schools, because as Brooks (2006) pointed out, the role of the tutor was much different from that of the teacher supporting the student on teaching practice. Teachers did not always have the time or appropriate expertise to support students when their main concern had still to be the children in the classroom. As the work of the CATE committee progressed throughout the decade, it became obvious that, with a few modest changes, the majority of courses in the 90 plus institutions were satisfying CATE criteria. Less than 4 per cent of institutions had to make major changes to their provision (Becher, 1992).

By 1990 it was generally accepted that the CATE system was helpful in providing independent scrutiny of courses and ensuring that there was some coordination of provision and accountability. After 1990 the CATE criteria were modified somewhat, to give local committees a more substantial role in scrutinising courses. During this period, CATE and the institutions had to take account of another significant change in schools which influenced their training courses – the National Curriculum, introduced by the education secretary Kenneth Baker.

In 1989, Kenneth Baker completed his term as education secretary (1986–9). During this time his attention had been mainly focussed on the Education Reform Act (1988) and the National Curriculum, which provided significant challenges to teacher training programmes. In many cases, courses had to be rewritten to include all aspects of that curriculum. Subsequently, they had to be approved by the validation panels of universities and then pass scrutiny by CATE officials. Nevertheless, despite the concern about course content which had continued for the past 25 years, it was not until the Carter Review of Teacher Training (DfE, 2015) that a recommendation was made to establish a framework of core content for ITT.

School-based training

The process by which most teacher training was carried out under the guidance of HE continued for a time, in spite of politically motivated calls for their role to end or be significantly reduced (Ribbins and Sherratt, 1997). Members of the Thatcher government, including education secretary Kenneth Baker, felt that staff involved in teacher training were motivating prospective teachers to be anti-government (Baker, 1993) and that they could be better trained on the job in schools (Browne and Reid 2012). Teacher training became a very political issue and for many commentators, ideological dogma and prejudice was seen to take the place of reason, argument and evidence (Mahony and Hextall, 2000). As a consequence of this pressure, the training of teachers was placed under further inspection and assessment, scrutiny which was seen by many as designed to endorse the right-wing prejudice which existed (Carr and Hartnett, 1996).

After much of the training had been moved into schools, comments by the Teacher Training Agency's (TTA) successor the Teacher Development Agency (TDA, 2006) and Furlong et al. (2000) may be seen to imply the existence of a political bias, although the need for more involvement of schools in the process was not without influential supporters elsewhere. For example, Professor Tim Brighouse, distinguished chief education officer of several local authorities, noted in an interview for this book in 2014 that in the 1980s he had been instrumental in involving schools in Oxfordshire in teacher training because he felt that it had been too college-based.

Kenneth Baker was also convinced that courses were too theoretical and paid too little attention to classroom practice (Ribbins and Sherratt, 1997). He had supported the development in 1989 of innovative schemes such as the Licenced Teacher Scheme, the Articled Teacher Scheme and indeed any initiative to increase the time trainee teachers spent in schools. These programmes were continued by his successors and were eventually amalgamated into the Graduate Teacher Scheme (GTS) in 1997.

The Licenced Teacher Scheme required students to be at least 26 years old, to have had two years studying in HE and to have passed GCSE in maths and English. It was used mainly in areas of teacher shortage, in many instances to recruit overseas qualified graduates into teaching. The trainee had to be employed for a minimum of two years by a local authority, which applied to central government for a grant to fund the programme. Trainees had to work predominantly with one school but also gain experience within another – at least 80 per cent of their time had to be spent working in school. Take-up was slow, but delivery of the grant was also slow. Questions asked in the House of Lords in spring 1990 (House of Lords Debate, 1990), revealed that only 55 applications had been made in the first six months. None had received grants six months later.

The Articled Teacher Scheme required students to be enrolled on a PGCE course and was similar in many respects to the Licenced Teacher Scheme. Both required a partnership between schools and HE with teachers in schools being mentors to the trainees. It was funded by grants, £5,000 for the first year and £6,000 for the second year. Extra bursaries were available for students opting to teach shortage subjects. Supply cover was made available to schools to cover mentoring and since the quality of mentoring was critical, mentor training was delivered by the training institution to schoolteachers. The perception grew that, because the scheme started at much the same time as the National Curriculum, the mentors were in fact experiencing their own professional development as they learned to become familiar with the new demands of the curriculum and assessment. The staff of one Berkshire secondary school where an Articled Teacher trainee was employed were initially enthused by a speech given by the education secretary at a conference (Fletcher, 1995). He said that teachers in classrooms 'know what they are doing and have the time to do it well'.

When the programme started, however, the teachers realised that time and resources were in fact scarce. The whole department in a secondary school had to be involved in the programme. Every teacher had to be prepared to help, in order to ensure that the trainee did not feel that their role was to provide 'cheap labour'. The mentor was 'learning on the job' (Fletcher, 1995), as a whole teaching and learning programme had to be planned. At its best, the scheme could add considerable value to the school and individuals concerned, but it was a complex and difficult process. The mentor could become the most important influence on a trainee teacher as he/she developed their experience (Elliott and Calderhead, 1994; Hobson and Malderez, 2002). However, that support was likely to be varied, with a possibly significant negative impact on the trainee (Ofsted, 2003; Hankey, 2004).

In primary schools the situation was similar. In Lancashire nine primary teachers acting as mentors in the Articled Teacher Scheme were interviewed about their roles in mentoring. They felt that much time had to be spent on fostering communication between those participating and that the skills to enable this were difficult to acquire (Davies and Harrison, 1995). Developing curriculum expertise, assessment techniques and teaching skills in a trainee was very difficult and there were doubts about whether practising teachers were really best placed to act as teacher trainers, unless they had comprehensive training and support. The quality of mentoring for trainee teachers has been an ongoing issue and the proper resourcing and comprehensive training of mentors remains an issue (DfE, 2015).

Research into school-based training

In view of the fact that some researchers into teacher training were based in the very institutions which were losing control of teacher training, their conclusions might sometimes be seen as biased. Researchers, however, attempted to ensure that they gave the best possible opportunity for school-based teacher training to be studied in an impartial light. Hannan (1995) surveyed nearly 500 primary schools in Devon to find out about their attitudes to the proposals to shift teacher training away from HE and centre it in schools. The majority of headteachers, parents, students and teachers were in favour of students spending an increased amount of time in schools, with many favouring a transfer of resources to schools from institutions. This latter finding was particularly supported by schools which already took on a significant role in training as a partnership school. However, schools wanted reassurance that as school-based training developed, there would be adequate resources to do the job properly. Unless the resource base was adequate, there was general opposition to the idea of schools taking the lead in the process. The research concluded by pointing out that few primary schools had demonstrated a wish to undertake the lead role in training and that in those secondary schools where increased partnership had been tried, there was a reluctance to continue the process.

In January 1993, an article in the *Independent* newspaper (MacLeod, 1993) noted that Ofsted was not wholeheartedly supportive of school-based training, pointing out that it was not a process which could be introduced quickly. The trainees all needed experience of at least two schools – schools in which all staff needed thorough preparation for their roles in relation to the training. Ofsted (1993a and 1993b) found that, in some instances, trainees who had gone through the Articled Teacher Scheme had very limited subject knowledge in National Curriculum subjects, although in general the new teachers had reached the same standard as those who had completed a PGCE in an institution. Monitoring of school-based students was likely to be poor. The school-based trainees, however, had more knowledge of schools and the role of the teacher than their 'institution-based' colleagues.

Two Modes of Teacher Education programmes, referred to as MOTE 1 and MOTE 2, were set up in 1991 and 1993 by the Economic and Social Research Council (Furlong et al., 2000). They ran until 1996 and their objective was to evaluate the moves towards greater involvement of schools and the shift of training to a predominantly school-based model. The authors refer to the ideological struggle between the government and others who had an interest in teacher education. The results of the research suggested that the Articled Teacher Scheme was generally seen as satisfactory, but variability of subject knowledge gave concern.

However, the Licensed Teacher Scheme was used by some LEAs and schools as a quick means to solve recruitment problems. Many entrants were employed in London and there was good representation of minority groups amongst entrants. Placements could be unsatisfactory with students often getting experience rather than training.

This type of training, however, was at least twice as expensive as training in HE (MacLeod, 1993) and the education secretary, Kenneth Clarke, decided to end the Articled Teacher Scheme for secondary students in 1992. Nevertheless, the majority of training funds were to be moved from HE to schools, to encourage the expansion of school-based courses.

Confirming the research discussed in this chapter, MacBeath would conclude later that the argument for school-based training was based on the assumption that schools which could provide a suitable environment for teacher education had satisfied a number of criteria and could be called 'genuine learning communities' (MacBeath, 2012). He suggested that there was much to do before schools reached that ideal and that, consequently, the role of universities in teacher education ought to have enhanced importance.

The Teacher Training Agency

Reform continued and there was pressure to increase the amount of time trainees from HE spent in classrooms. Eventually, proposals were put forward that the time spent in schools was to be 80 per cent of a course (although this was later reduced to 66 per cent). At the same time, ideas were beginning to be formulated for a new Ofsted framework and a new quango to succeed CATE. The secretary of state, John Patten, wanted the new organisation to dictate funding and oversee the quality assessment of training. He was supported in this by the prime minister, John Major. He felt that teacher training as a whole was in need of reform. He emphasised the importance of training in schools and favoured the idea of linking quality assessment to funding provision (Major, 1999). The Education Act of 1994 was intended to enable this, under the guidance of a new secretary of state, Gillian Shephard, and CATE was eventually superseded by the TTA in 1994, which had a wider remit than CATE.

Under this regime, all courses were to be funded at the same rate, with funding linked to the quality of provision and with the TTA determining the balance of provision between school-based and HE-based training. The appointment to the TTA board of two outspoken supporters of school-based training was indicative of the political mood of the times (Carr and Hartnett, 1996).

Government control of education was further emphasised by the introduction of a new National Curriculum for teacher training set out in Circular 4/98 (DfEE, 1998a), which emphasised aspects of subject knowledge.

When the continuing shortage of teachers gave concern, performance-related pay was introduced – a device used in private corporations and now seen as the answer to teacher-recruitment problems (Ball, 2008). In the opinion of John

Major, all public services could be improved by the introduction of private enterprise (Major, 1999) and Gillian Shephard saw the brief of the TTA as developing and managing a 'market' for the provision of teacher training (Abbott et al., 2013). It was argued that this would increase the involvement of schools and encourage a diversity of routes into the profession. It could also commission research with the object of improving the standard of training.

Inspecting ITT

To enable funding to follow quality, an independent inspectorate was needed, to develop a new inspection framework, and Ofsted, the organisation which inspected schools, was required to take on the task. The organisation began to inspect providers of teacher education in 1994 using standards set by the TTA. These included standards related to teaching the National Curriculum, developing teaching skills and supporting teachers in their roles as mentors in the classroom. Schools and newly qualified teachers were also inspected as part of the process.

Chris Woodhead, the first chief executive of Ofsted, was regarded with great suspicion in schools, because of his habit of criticising schools using what seemed to be dubious statistics, which received wide publicity in the popular press (Davies, 2000). He had strongly supported the right-wing agenda attacking teacher education and when Ofsted began to inspect teacher education, he was always likely to be unpopular in training institutions. Institutions which did well when inspected were given the opportunity to recruit more students, whereas the opposite applied to institutions not seen to be meeting the required standards. This clearly defined market philosophy only broke down when the institutions deemed to be doing well could not cope with the growing numbers, in which case lower-performing providers were needed to take up the extra places.

The TTA made definite attempts to support training separate from HE institutions. In 1994/5 the author was working for a Midlands university and was regularly asked by local education committees to attend inspectors' meetings, where HE links with local schools and teachers were discussed. A senior TTA officer was present at one meeting in 1995. She expressed disapproval when informed of the long-standing link between the LEA and university, and asked that the university representative be excluded – to the obvious embarrassment of the LEA officers present. It subsequently transpired that the discussion had centred upon increasing school-based training and the start of the School-Centred Initial Teacher Training (SCITT) (see below) in the local authority. When the project eventually started, the LEA asked the university for advice on how to develop a SCITT, and paid the university out of TTA funds for the advice.

LEAs were glad to have a government agency suggesting that projects of school-based training like SCITT could be staffed by advisors and inspectors rather than HE staff, because there had been a determined initiative by the Conservative government to take power away from local authorities (Abbott et al., 2013) which had brought threats of redundancy to LEA officers.

School-Centred Initial Teacher Training

In 1995 the TTA began to establish SCITT, which theoretically did not require the involvement of HE. The SCITT route (under a variety of guises) into teaching still continues in 2018 and, although there have been various changes, the basics remain much as they were originally.

A SCITT programme, is a school-based way into teaching, which was originally 'sold' on the Department for Education website as being 'less academic'. A SCITT can be started by individual schools or LEAs in consortia, who recruit suitably qualified graduates to train to become qualified teachers under their guidance. Some consortia have been in operation since the programme began and may involve many schools and several LEAs. They can involve the independent sector and even local further education institutions. Students complete most of their training in one school but do further practice in others. The majority of the training is carried out in schools, but the training can lead to a PGCE validated by HE, which in some cases can give credit towards a master's degree. Students have to pay fees, but a variety of bursaries and grants are available.

The Graduate Teacher Scheme

For those schools and LEAs which did not want to take full responsibility for setting up SCITT training, the GTS was proposed by the TTA in 1996, and begun two years later. Applicants had to be graduates aged at least 24, with qualifications relevant to their chosen age group and subject. The minimum length of the programme was 13 weeks, although most were expected to continue for a year. After changes in 2000, it developed into a system whereby the trainee was employed by a school as an extra member of staff and paid a salary which, together with a training grant, was paid by the TTA. This development encouraged more schools to participate. Priority categories of shortage subjects were also introduced. Successful completion of the programme led to the award of a PGCE. Applicants for the GTS had initially to find a school willing to employ them, and a training plan had to be set up in conjunction with a recommending body. This could be a HE provider or a SCITT. The plan had to be approved by the TTA, but its implementation was the responsibility of the recommending body. The GTS stopped recruiting in 2012.

1997–2010

Education, education, education

As has been seen, there was an ideological basis on the part of the Conservative government for many of the initiatives which evolved during the period between 1979 and 1997. They were strongly supported by the controversial chief inspector of schools, Chris Woodhead (Gillard, 2011). When the Labour Party gained power in the election of 1997, the training programmes set up earlier were continued. Indeed, a report written in 2006 by the TDA, the successor to the TTA, noted (paras 3–4) with apparent self-satisfaction that its chief executive in 2000 had called it one of the best market-management systems in government and that Ruth Kelly, a Labour secretary of state for education (2004–6), had praised its modernising practices. In contrast, HE had seen the TTA as confrontational because of a lack of consultation and the fact that the practices which it endorsed led to teachers becoming 'technicians' rather than reflective professionals (McKenzie, 2001). The increase in paperwork generated by the TTA, and later the TDA, was seen as a bureaucratic nightmare by staff working in HE. Partly as a result of this, some institutions that had always seen the training teachers as one of their main academic tasks now began to feel that, in order to be certain of financial stability in the future, they had to diversify their range of programmes.

As noted previously, Worcester had been founded as an emergency training centre after the war and its work had always centred around the education of teachers. Between 2003 and 2008, under a business-orientated vice chancellor, it expanded far beyond the training of teachers, with the aim of becoming a university (Cheesewright, 2008). This aim was achieved in 2005 and, under a Labour government, it aimed to provide a wide range of degrees and vocational courses to other professions. The number of students rose to over 8,000.

At the Warwick Institute of Education, tutors noticed the increased control by government over the curriculum and assessment, and the focus of the Institute of Education shifted from teacher training to more general research-based activity (Abbott, 2008). There was resentment that since the last decade of the twentieth century, teaching as a research-based profession had ceased to be part of the debate on teacher training and a 'common-sense approach' informed by political ideology was now commonplace (McNicholl et al., 2013). Carr and Hartnett (1996) noted that, in this period, enlightened thinking about education was derided. Even where partnership models had been developed, such as the University of Warwick, where tutors had felt an effective model had been introduced, the time and effort to manage and document such a programme was becoming excessive. HE tutors now began to feel that their time might be better spent on research rather than training – obviously a most important facet of work in a research-focussed university (Abbott, 2008).

With the craft-based approach to teacher education continuing, the decision was taken in 2007 to end the Warwick Bachelor of Arts with Qualified Teacher Status, which had originated in the Teaching Certificate. Four hundred places were lost, but the institute continued primary and secondary PGCE courses. The Warwick GTS recruited just over 50 students in 2008 and attempts were made to tempt students from across the university to try teaching via the Student Associates Scheme. In line with a national effort (TDA, 2006), students were recruited to programmes for students wishing to work with younger children. A degree in early childhood studies was started with places for 50 students.

St Mary's in Cheltenham went through a series of changes including two amalgamations as it attempted to maintain a role for teacher training within the HE sector. By 2001 it was part of the University of Gloucester, which had approaching 10,000 students in 2010. Students could still train to be schoolteachers, or follow a more general course of education studies. The college's traditional strength in preparing teachers for younger primary pupils was still evident and, like Warwick, they took advantage of the TDA's support for courses in this field.

At the millennium, there was a significant shortage of applicants to teaching, a situation which school-based courses had been supposed to alleviate. Application figures did increase, but between 2000 and 2001, out of almost 5,000 trainees in the shortage subjects of science and maths, less than 20 per cent were in the school-based schemes (TDA, 2006).

Unfortunately, not many schools were willing to participate in school-based training, and many that did so became involved in order to solve a particular issue within their school – for example, where a secondary school was having difficulty in recruiting foreign-language teachers and an interested parent was a foreign-language graduate. Or in Warwickshire, where a trainee successfully worked through a tailored Graduate Teacher Programme organised by the Institute of Education at Warwick, after having been a headteacher in South Africa. Other GTS trainees in the same county were graduates who were working voluntarily in primary schools which their own children attended. They wished to become part-time teachers in the locality. Many trainees across the country were overseas-trained staff, or teachers from further education who wished to develop their existing qualifications. Although it was evident that schemes like the GTS could attract committed and enthusiastic mature entrants, it added proportionally few to the teaching force.

Researching the Graduate Teacher Scheme

Research pointed to some mixed results in the GTS which are set out below (Foster, 2001; Ofsted, 2002). Funding was seen as generous and selection processes satisfactory. Schools generally were positive about the outcomes, with most trainees showing real commitment to their main school. Trainees reached a satisfactory level of competence in all the standards but Ofsted was disappointed, because many of them had the potential to do better and were not reaching the higher standards of which they were thought to be capable.

Trainees were able to make a significant contribution and the schools could make a realistic assessment of the potential of the teacher if they were considering offering employment at the end of the programme. Trainees were salaried members of staff and so had prestige within their schools. Participating in the scheme meant that existing staff members experienced significant staff development, as they planned and implemented training programmes. However, there was uncertainty amongst some schools and staff about how to plan and implement teacher training programmes, especially in relation to time management. The first duty of the teachers was still to the pupils in their care.

The school-based training with one school as the main centre of training limited the trainee's knowledge of a wide range of teaching environments. There was often a lack of other trainees with whom to discuss their experiences. When problems occurred on school practice organised by HE, the trainee could be moved to a different environment. In the GTS, trainees and their schools did not have that facility. The shortage of teachers in specific subjects was not helped by these schemes.

There was concern that, in some instances, the assessment of graduate teachers was not as rigorous as for trainees gaining their qualifications via other routes. Teachers in schools were often uncertain about the assessment of trainees and, in addition, the nature of the partnership and involvement of the trainee in the school community could lead to difficulties when teachers were required to make dispassionate judgements which had enormous influence on the future of the trainee. Ofsted was particularly concerned about this aspect of assessment when the trainee was on the pass/fail borderline.

Recommending bodies, who were responsible for the programme followed by trainees, were in charge of assessment. In some instances, their own monitoring programmes were not keeping pace with the number of trainees using the route. Rigorous scrutiny of their own processes was rare. Generally, however, schools which did train teachers via the GTS were satisfied with the results, though it was clear that the newly qualified teacher and the mentor had to carry an immense responsibility during the programme.

A revised approach to teacher shortages

As the Labour government pressed ahead with the manifesto sound bite of 'education, education, education', more funding was committed to schools and improving children's welfare. A Sure Start programme in 1999 and the National Childcare Strategy in 1998 were evidence of this commitment. However, the election manifesto had little to say about teacher training. The newly formed Standards and Effectiveness Unit had it in their remit but the TTA continued to have real responsibility.

A quinquennial review led by the TTA in 1999 noted the falling supply of recruits and the shortage of serving teachers and, in response, the government was very generous in allocating funds to tackle the problem (TDA, 2006). Consequently, the TTA developed a new strategy of funding, by initiating a national advertising campaign and offering bursaries of between 4,000 and 6,000 pounds to lure people into the profession. The particular emphasis was on trying to allay the shortage of staff in mathematics and the sciences. In these subjects the campaign was particularly successful and in general the number of trainees began to improve. Between 2001 and 2005 numbers almost doubled. There were now a variety of different ways of gaining qualified teacher status, including:

1. an assessment only process for those who had taught in schools for a time without formal qualification;
2. a route for overseas-trained teachers whose qualifications were not recognised in the United Kingdom.

The vast majority of new entrants, however, still came via training in institutions of HE. In 1998 a green paper, 'Meeting the Challenge of Change' (DfEE, 1998a), was published under the auspices of David Blunkett, the secretary of state. It pointed out that new standards and specific content requirements for teacher training would be in place by 1999. The TTA could withdraw accreditation of a provider, but there was still a need to be certain that all who gained qualified teacher status were of a sufficient standard. This led to a computerised skills test being introduced by the TTA, which had to be passed by all who wanted to gain qualified teacher status. There were three parts – numeracy, literacy and ICT – which could be completed in any of 50 test centres in England. The candidates had to attain a mark of 60 per cent to pass and could take the test as often as they wished. Until it was passed, candidates who went into teaching could only be paid on an unqualified basis. The green paper also focussed attention on strengthening and extending employment-based routes into the profession. The Teaching and Higher Education Act of 1998 (DfEE, 1998a, 1998b) enabled the inspection of teacher training by HMI.

Teach First

It was suspected that some graduates could be tempted to try teaching, provided they were given the opportunity to leave if the profession proved not to suit their needs. An American initiative was introduced in England in 2002, which became known as Teach First in the United Kingdom and continues to recruit, although with some changes from the original format. The adoption of Teach First was partly as a result of businesses trying to help improve secondary education in London, but subsequently spread across the United Kingdom.

Graduates with a 'good' degree in specific subjects were recruited from the 'best universities'. They were initially awarded an unqualified teacher salary and, after the first year in school, moved on to a higher salary. Mentoring was carried out by business personnel, school leaders, teachers in the school and university staff. A two-year Leadership Development Scheme was employed which was seen to be relevant inside schools or, if used outside schools, in other businesses. Trainees (or participants in Teach First parlance) began with a summer school of six weeks in a university to prepare them for the classroom. They then worked in a school for two years. The university tutors worked with them to achieve PGCE and qualified teacher status. Credits towards a master's degree could also be awarded to trainees. The TDA, which succeeded the TTA in 2005, suggested that the scheme raised the profile of teaching as a product and in that respect it was seen as a success. However, a high proportion of the trainees did not enter the teaching profession and, in evidence submitted to a Parliamentary Education Committee in 2012, it was said to be expensive compared to traditional PGCE routes (HC Oral Evidence, 2012). We will return to look at Teach First in more detail in later chapters.

The Training and Development Agency

The Labour governments in this period were certainly more conciliatory towards the traditional teacher training institutions, who were given access to more funding. The amount of TTA- and TDA-driven bureaucracy was curtailed – in some instances being cut by 90 per cent. It was accepted that there ought to be scope for experienced training providers to show initiative, rather than follow a 'one-size-fits-all' approach. New standards were formulated and Ofsted changed their procedures. As the changes occurred, the TTA became less focussed on recruitment and was seen as a vehicle of development. The title of the organisation was changed to the TDA by the 2005 Education Act (DfEE, 2005).

Initially, the intention was for board members of the new organisation (some of whom were government appointees) to have some experience of education, but this was repealed. Nevertheless, the organisation was to work more closely with schools, but continued to have teacher training and recruitment as a concern.

The changes were broadly welcomed within the teaching profession, although it would appear that some of the ideas perpetrated by the TTA under the Labour government elected in 2001 seemed to demonstrate a rather limited view of schools. The TDA report of 2006, for example, extols the development of a new initiative *to encourage schools to develop a child-centred team* approach. Although a 'tick box' culture had been evident in some schools, many teachers and teacher trainers had not succumbed to the type of management theories which had encouraged league tables and 'naming and shaming' of schools in difficulty. They had always followed a child-centred approach.

Schools were now to be seen as places where all personnel, from catering and security staff to teachers and teaching assistants, were expected to contribute to the education of pupils. Most schools, particularly primary schools, had never deviated from this approach.

The TDA continued to promote a variety of routes by which aspiring teachers could gain qualified teacher status, including:

- The undergraduate and PGCE routes provided by HE institutions.
- Employment-based approaches including Teach First and SCITT training. An assessment-only route was also available if required.

Ofsted monitored the quality of newly qualified staff who had qualified through any route and, after their training was completed, teachers had to be effective in their work and committed to the schools and the children in their charge.

The Labour manifesto had promised to increase the number of teachers and from 2001 to 2010 the numbers increased significantly. The previous Conservative administrations had made little financial investment in state education and although financial restraints were now eased, there was a continued commitment to increase standards, develop a market philosophy and maintain centralised control of the curriculum, assessment and teacher training.

The TDA website was set up soon after the quango came into being and, as has been mentioned above, was seen as another way of raising the profile of 'the brand'. The teaching profession had indeed become a commercial product to sell to students. The website set out in detail the methods by which candidates could enter teaching and specified precisely what would be required of the trainee and the providing institution. For example, the four-year HE course had to provide 32 weeks in school, two- and three-year courses 24 weeks, secondary PGCE courses 24 weeks and primary PGCE 18 weeks. In each case, experience of two schools was necessary. Knowledge of the National Curriculum programmes of study was needed, as was an ability to set learning objectives, manage classes and know about behaviour-management techniques. An awareness of the professional values of teachers was also specified. This website indicated clearly what the Cambridge Review (Alexander et al., 2010) later criticised as the one-size-fits-all model of teaching.

Nevertheless, the website also included much information helpful to trainee teachers and the profession as a whole. Funding provision was set out clearly and opportunities for professional development considered. Good practice in ITT and in schools was identified and set out as an aid to teacher trainers and schoolteachers.

Towards the election of 2010

In 2007, after criticism of aspects of childhood in Britain by UNICEF, 'The Children's Plan' was published under the auspices of Ed Balls, the secretary of state for children, schools and families (DfES, 2007). The plan included reference to the need for newly qualified teachers to have master's-level qualifications, as a move towards a profession in which all teachers were qualified at a higher level. A desire was expressed to improve the training of teachers of children with special needs and to recruit 100,000 more teachers before the election in 2010 (para 4.15). There was to be a continued focus on classroom skills and the GTS was to be improved.

A year prior to the publishing of 'The Children's Plan', the Cambridge Primary Review was launched. Led by Robin Alexander, one of the authors of the 'Three Wise Men' report (Alexander et al., 1992), it was carried out at much the same time as a review of the primary curriculum prepared by another of the 'Wise Men', Jim Rose. This was called the 'Independent Report of the Primary Curriculum' (IRPC) (DCSF, 2009) although it was carried out for the government.

The secretary of state had wanted to introduce changes to the primary curriculum in 2011, and opponents of the government saw the review as an attempt to deflect attention from adverse headlines generated by the Cambridge Review as it progressed. Although the TDA contributed towards the IRPC, there was little specific reference to ITT when it reported in 2009. Nevertheless, some of the findings could have had important implications for those training new teachers. For example, cross-curricula work was advocated and the value of play in the development of social skills in children's learning was noted – ideas that in their broadest sense had been dismissed by most of the politicians who had held power since the 1970s.

In order to enable teachers to introduce this new policy, the report pointed out that training would be required for serving teachers. This implied that their original training had certainly been lacking. To the observer there were hints of the four disciplines of education referred to in Chapter 3 as 'education studies'.

To many, the IRPC could not be seen as independent of government, because the secretary of state had set it up and professionals had not contributed. Indeed, it was largely seen as the work of one man (Gillard, 2011). The Cambridge Review was truly independent and did have specific points to make about teacher training, which were certainly unpopular in both of the main political parties. It reflected on the fact that a student could train for between one year and four years – either in HE or in a school. It criticised the increased level of prescription from the centre, particularly the controlling of the curriculum and assessment. The fact that the TTA and the TDA saw themselves as successful was discounted, because these quangos were only assessing teaching quality against criteria which they themselves had set up and which the review felt were inadequate. Indeed, centrally dictated teacher training as a whole was seen as inadequate, because no consideration was given to the purpose or value of education. Personal judgement on the part of the teacher and the need to enquire critically into educational processes was not encouraged by the TDA. The emphasis instead was on delivering national strategies, with the use of mechanistic techniques where compliance with central *diktat* was seen as being more important than engagement with children. Central control had led to an approach to teaching in which all teachers were expected to use the same basic strategies throughout their career. Individual flair and any eccentricity (which the review suggested might inspire the pupils) were to be avoided.

The IRPC and the Cambridge Review came to very different conclusions in terms of what the primary school curriculum should consist of, but both came to nothing in terms of influencing future policy, though for very different reasons (Abbott et al., 2013). The Independent Review was accepted by the Labour government, which was to lose the election of 2010. When it was rejected by the Coalition government which gained power, it was consigned to history. The Cambridge Review provoked vigorous debate amongst academics, teachers and politicians, but was also rejected by the Coalition government which came into power.

Conclusion

This chapter describes the transfer of control of teacher education from institutions of HE to central government of whatever colour. Between 1979 and 2010, aspects of the teaching profession, including teacher training, became part of the ideological struggle between the advocates of a market-driven, competition-led approach to public services and those who maintained that such an approach could be too mechanistic and value-free to be of use in schools and in teacher training.

A number of government quangos and a system of inspection of training provision was introduced during the period, as vigorous attempts were made by central government to move teacher training back to a classroom-based system in schools and improve recruitment. Outside agencies, including private providers, were encouraged to access funding and several new school-based approaches were started, which both Labour and Conservative governments supported. However, as a result of the apparent desire of government to diminish their role, traditional providers of teacher training in universities and colleges began to withdraw from teacher training.

5

CURRENT GOVERNMENT POLICY

Introduction

In the previous chapters we have traced the historical development of teacher education in England, culminating in the growth of a competitive market, with the introduction of a number of different providers and the relative decline of the involvement and influence of higher education (HE). In this chapter, we will consider how current policy has built on this strategy and led to the development of a number of different training routes being made available to those wishing to train as teachers. Set alongside this process has been the continued reform of the school system, with the establishment of free schools and the continued growth of the academies programme.

The apparent deregulation of the school system with a large number of organisations becoming involved in the control and running of schools has contributed to a culture where schools are more confident about their ability to provide a range of functions without the involvement of external organisations such as local authorities or universities. This deregulation has been supported by a greater emphasis on the importance of subject knowledge for teachers, which has been reflected in the introduction of new curriculum and assessment regimes in schools. There has been a corresponding increased emphasis on trainee teachers having appropriate subject knowledge, which can be developed by practical experience gained by working with experienced teachers in school, rather than through HE institutions.

Political context

Education has become a major political issue and there has been a great deal of debate about the way in which education should be provided and how the system should be organised. The election of a minority Conservative government supported by the Liberal Democratic Party in 2010 led to a shift from the previous

Labour government's policies. Over the previous 25 years, as we have outlined in the previous chapters, the overall policy focus remained on a market-led, competition-led approach to the provision of public services. The new government continued this process, but the Coalition government led by David Cameron placed an increased emphasis on the importance of individual schools and the role of individual headteachers in bringing about improvements in the education system, and moved away from an integrated children's service (Abbott et al., 2013; DfE, 2010). Within teacher education there was continued political pressure to marginalise the role played by HE institutions and to increase the role played by schools in the training process (Furlong, 2013; Whitty, 2014). The majority Conservative governments, led by David Cameron between 2015 and 2016 and by Theresa May between 2016 and 2017, and the subsequent May minority government supported by Northern Ireland's Democratic Unionist Party, all stressed the importance of subject knowledge, practical experience, policy implementation, a range of providers and schools being at the forefront of the process in the development and implementation of teacher education policy (DfE, 2010; Gove, 2010; Carter, 2015; DfE, 2016b; 2016c). The attack on the role of HE in the training of teachers and the attempts to reduce their involvement has been sustained and has led to major restructuring within the system. However, the importance of the major role played by teachers and the significance of high-quality teachers in securing a 'world-class' education system has been consistently emphasised by successive governments during this period (for example see DfE, 2010; DfE, 2016c). There is a recognition by government of the importance of ensuring high-quality entrants into the teaching profession. The government considers this can be best achieved through the approach to teacher education it have developed, with schools being placed at the centre of the process. Beckett and Nuttall (2017: 623) claim that these are 'fragmented and impoverished policies of recent years, not just in England but internationally, that prevents practising teachers and academic partners working together'. We will return in detail to the ways in which schools and HE work together in later chapters and there is still evidence of close cooperation, but the relationship between the different parties has changed. As we noted in previous chapters, the ability of teacher educators to influence policy and to direct the debate has been consistently reduced by the impact of government initiatives.

There is a belief on the part of the government that teachers who are grounded in practice and who are kept away from theory will be able to raise standards in schools. This does not preclude the use of evidence-based practice which promotes particular approaches to teaching, but the emphasis on practice results in a reluctance to utilise research (see for example Furlong and Oancea, 2005; BERA-RSA, 2014). There has been a succession of centrally devised and delivered policies that claim to be evidence-based and which promote particular ways of working, without recognising there might be alternative approaches that are more appropriate to the circumstances and context. Throughout this period, since 2010, there has been an ongoing drive in England to raise school standards and to create a 'world-class system', and according to the government:

> We have no choice but to be radical if our ambition is to be world class. The most successful countries already combine a high status teaching profession, high levels of autonomy for schools, a comprehensive and effective accountability system and a strong sense of aspiration for all children, whatever their background.
>
> (DfE, 2010: 4–5)

It is easy to see how the reforms introduced to teacher education fit into this narrative, although there is a strong acknowledgement that a key component of any successful education system is the quality of the teaching profession. What is a matter of debate is, what is the most effective way of training teachers to ensure the high-quality teaching that the government is striving for? We will consider the actual routes and ways in which the government aims to achieve this later in the chapter.

These changes and policy debates have been taking place against a background of severe austerity following the financial crisis, with major reductions in public expenditure. Schools in particular have faced significant reductions in their budget and headteachers have been forced to make difficult choices about how they utilise their resources (National Association of Headteachers, 2018). The broader political context has been dominated by the debate surrounding the decision to leave the European Union following the 2016 referendum. At this point this has not had a direct impact on education policy but Brexit has led to, in 2017, the election of a minority government and several ministerial changes in the Department for Education (DfE). This has resulted in a relative period of policy inertia and a reduction in the scale and pace of policy reform as the government has been focussed on delivering Brexit and has also been dogged by infighting within its own members about the terms of the United Kingdom's (UK) exit from the European Union. However, the direction of policy, outlined earlier in the chapter, remains the same and earlier initiatives such as reforming the school curriculum and the introduction of new assessment regimes are now coming into effect in schools (BBC, 2018).

Carter Review

The Carter Review was commissioned by the then secretary of state for education Michael Gove and reported in 2015. Whilst setting out the importance of working in partnership, the trends we have highlighted in the previous section are clear to see. Carter (2015: 3) argues:

> Possible debates around whether ITT should be delivered by School-Centred Initial Teacher Training providers (SCITTs) or universities, School Direct or not, are not terribly helpful in this process. The truth is that partnership is the key. Sometimes universities will take the lead, sometimes and increasingly, it

idea that teachers are researchers of their own practice who continue to develop through their career.

(Carter, 2015: 22)

There has certainly been an increase in the importance of educational research and evidence-based practice since the period during the 1990s when any sort of theoretical input was being heavily discouraged by government policy. The DfE has been keen to increase the use of evidence-based research into education (Goldacre, 2013). The DfE has also funded the Sutton Trust to set up the Education Endowment Fund, to develop strategies to help 'teachers to find and use the most effective teaching methods to improve standards for all children, including the most disadvantaged' (DfE, 2016c: 38).

As part of this process to support greater use of evidence in education, there has been a reduced emphasis on the role of academic staff from university departments of education. This has involved the increased use of outside agencies such as the Sutton Trust and other university departments not normally associated with teacher education. This raises a wider issue about the continued role of university departments of education in teacher education. The various benchmarking exercises designed to measure the quality of research in universities, for example the 2014 Research Excellence Framework (REF), has tended to result in the relatively small-scale research undertaken by staff in schools of education to be considered to be more limited than research in more high-profile departments. According to Andrew Pollard who chaired the education panel for the 2014 REF:

> The activity required to compete successfully in social scientific terms is, in my opinion, becoming increasingly distinct from the activity required to flourish in the rapidly changing field of teacher education. The pressure which this puts on staff working in education is sometimes extremely acute.
>
> *(Pollard, 2014: 2)*

This will create additional pressures for some departments, especially those in research-intensive universities, where there is increased pressure for research to be internationally significant. When this is added to pressures relating to student recruitment, given the competition from a variety of providers, many universities have been considering their future involvement in teacher education (see for example Peiser 2016). A recent example of the radical restructuring that is taking place in HE is the reorganisation of the Institute of Education at the University of Warwick, which has established a strong record in research. The institute was replaced by two centres, the Centre for Education Studies, focussing on research and post-graduate work, and the Centre for Teacher Education, which has no research role and is solely concerned with teacher training. This restructuring was designed partly to deal with the impact of REF and to increase the opportunities for research for those staff who work in the Centre for Education Studies but who would have no involvement in teacher education.

While there is undoubtedly a renewed focus on the role of research in teacher education, it is not necessarily being provided by the traditional providers and this may be partly due to the long-standing suspicion of university departments of education, which, as we have reported in previous chapters, have often been accused of a left-wing bias. A great deal of the current education policy is still driven by the legacy of the secretary of state for education between 2010 and 2015, Michael Gove, who accused university departments of education of promoting 'ideologically driven theory' (Gove, 2013). The Carter Review, whilst supporting the role of research, emphasised a change in the provision and focus of educational research, which should focus on the support of enhanced classroom practice.

An important part of any teacher training system is the role played by school mentors who provide support to trainee teachers. Low-quality mentoring is likely to have an adverse impact on those training to be teachers. The Carter Review identified the characteristics of effective mentoring:

- Effective mentors are outstanding teachers who are also skilled in deconstructing and explaining their practice – outstanding practitioners are not automatically outstanding mentors.
- Effective mentors are subject and phase experts, aware of the latest developments. Subject mentors should be members of subject mentor networks and should access resources from subject associations.
- The most effective mentors have a secure understanding of the Teachers' Standards, including a range of methods for assessing against the standards, in a way that goes beyond the minimum requirements for meeting them.
- Effective mentors are strong role models of all the Teachers' Standards – for example, they are skilled in managing behaviour effectively. Effective mentors are also good role models in relation to their own engagement with research.
(Carter, 2015: 41)

It would be difficult to disagree with these characteristics and, especially from a trainee teacher perspective, the quality of mentoring is often crucial to a successful outcome. However, again there is strong reference to the Teachers' Standards and they reflect a certain orthodox approach. School-based mentors will inevitably promote the methods that are utilised within their own school and there is a danger that trainee teachers will not be encouraged to develop a range of strategies, or to challenge the status quo (see for example Mutton, 2016). Newly qualified teachers may lack the ability to challenge current orthodoxies and to adopt a range of approaches. This may be even more profound in training programmes run by multi-academy trusts (MATs) who promote a particular way of lesson preparation, teaching and learning approaches and assessment methods across all the schools in the MAT. There is a danger that 'professional knowledge becomes simplified, flattened, it is essentially about contemporary practice in schools' (Furlong et al., 2006: 41).

The Carter Review stresses the fundamental importance of mentors within a school-based system and recognises that effective training is required to overcome any potential inconsistencies in the system. Variations in the level of support provided by mentors has been a constant issue in the English system, which has come to heavily rely on the role of school mentors (Hobson et al., 2009). The findings of the Carter Review sum up a general approach to teacher education based on central control of the system, with a common system of standards, a variety of providers, the importance of schools in the process and a functional emphasis on classroom practice. There is a recognition of the value of evidence-based practice and a recognition that HE has a role to play. However, the individual school and their teachers are clearly identified as the key players in initial teacher education. In practice, the Carter Review was subsumed by the wider political events that we described earlier in the chapter, but the direction of travel it proposes continues, and it provides a useful template of the general reforms that have taken place in teacher education.

Routes and options

In earlier chapters, we identified the movement of teacher education to a school-based system and the development of a range of training routes. In Chapters 7 to 9 we will consider the provider and student responses to these programmes, but it is useful to give an indication of the main training routes available. There are still a limited number of undergraduate routes available, but the main focus is now on post-graduate provision and includes:

- Provider-led: where a tuition fee is payable to the accredited ITT provider to cover the cost of training. Training places are held by the ITT provider.
- School direct (fee): where a school partnership works with an ITT provider to which a tuition fee is payable to cover the cost of training. Training places are held by the school partnership.
- School direct (salaried): where a school partnership works with an ITT provider and the trainee is employed within the school partnership. Training places are held by the school partnership in which the trainee is employed.
- Post-graduate teaching apprenticeship: where a school partnership works with an ITT provider that is on the Register of Apprenticeship Providers and the apprentice is employed within the school partnership. Training places are held by the school partnership in which the apprentice is employed. (DfE, 2018a: 3)

Recruitment to the majority of subjects and routes is unlimited, whereas previously providers were given targets allocated by the DfE. Providers have to notify the DfE of the numbers they hope to recruit, to help the DFE to understand demand and capacity nationally. According to the DfE (2018a:6):

> When considering the minimum viability and maximum capacity of their training programmes, ITT providers and lead schools should account for their

most recent cohort sizes, recent recruitment patterns, current or anticipated growth in partnership arrangements, recent trends in applicant route preferences and a realistic assessment of employment needs in the local area. This applies to the capacity for training that their partnerships can accommodate and their ability to attract high quality trainees who will make excellent teachers.

Giving providers greater control of their recruitment and allowing significant local variation alongside a range of different routes and providers is a significant move towards a market-based system of teacher training. The decision to allow unlimited recruitment to programmes can be viewed as part of the continuing marketisation of teacher education and to encourage successful providers to expand. Rather than a national system, this will also increase the localised nature of provision. There appears to be a move towards a system which could lead to:

- the emergence of a 'system of many small systems';
- the complete deregulation of ITE;
- the ending of 'the core national professionalism associated with the QTS award'; and
- the emergence of 'local' and 'branded' professionalisms. (Whitty, 2014: 473)

However, there is also realisation that teacher shortages and a failure to retain teachers has contributed to a need to allow greater flexibility in the system, through a variety of routes and providers, although this is likely to contribute to some difficult planning decisions by the institutions involved in the process. The move towards a school-based system with many schools being allowed to run their own teacher training programmes has done little to alleviate the shortage in the number of people training to be teachers. Whilst successful schools have been able to train their own staff many less successful schools have found it difficult to train and recruit teaching staff.

There continues to be a crisis in teacher recruitment with, especially, a number of subject areas experiencing severe shortages, for example maths and science at secondary level, especially in the more deprived areas of England. According to Sibieta (2018: 6):

- Applications to teacher training were down by about 5 percent in 2018 as compared with the same point last year. Training targets have been persistently missed in maths and science.
- Exit rates have also crept up over time, from 8 to 9 percent in primary schools and from 9 to 10 per cent in secondary schools between 2011 and 2017.
- Exit rates are particularly high early in teachers' careers, with only 60 per cent of teachers working in a state-funded school in England five years after starting training.

There is a long-term crisis in recruitment which is exacerbated by the large number of teachers who leave the teaching profession, especially in their first five years of teaching, allied to rising pupil numbers in schools. There is a need for more teachers in schools just as the number of applicants for teacher training programmes is falling and increasing numbers are leaving the teaching profession (Sibieta, 2018). Whilst this problem cannot be blamed solely on teacher training policy, there are a number of additional reasons including teachers' pay and conditions of service. Government policy has failed to address this issue and a move towards a 'free market' in recruitment has done little to solve the problem of under-recruitment into the teaching profession. For some schools the situation has further deteriorated as they struggle to recruit sufficient numbers of specialist staff. In many schools graduates in other subject areas find themselves teaching maths and some science subjects.

Given these changes and problems, where is this direction of government policy leading teacher training? An extract from the white paper 'Educational Excellence Everywhere' (DfE, 2016a) illustrates how the government intended this approach to recruitment and training to work in practice:

> By 2020, a teacher's training may look like this (illustrative example):
>
> Chris graduates from university and gets into teaching through a School Direct course run by a multi academy trust that has been accredited to deliver school-based training. His initial training builds on the deep subject knowledge he acquired in his degree, and trains him in the most effective methods of teaching his specialist subject. It also gives him a firm grounding in understanding and applying evidence based practice.
>
> When he successfully completes his initial teacher training, Chris is employed to teach in one of the schools in the MAT where he trained. During his first year he has access to a package of support – a dedicated mentor, a reduced teaching timetable and tailored development opportunities (including opportunities to use and apply high quality evidence to support his development) to help him consolidate what he learnt in his initial training.
>
> In January of his second year in the classroom, Chris's mentor and head teacher judge that he is consistently meeting the Teachers' Standards at the required level. The head teacher makes a recommendation to a local teaching school authorised to act as an 'external examiner' for teachers seeking accreditation.
>
> The teaching school reviews Chris's practice and is satisfied that Chris is consistently demonstrating the required standard in his teaching. It therefore confirms accreditation and Chris becomes a fully accredited teacher.
>
> *(DfE, 2016a: 34)*

Under this model there is a clear pathway for the trainee teacher. They would work within a system that is heavily school-based and which is dependent on serving teachers to direct the training programme. Experience would be restricted to schools within the MAT which would be likely to adopt similar approaches and systems. There is a strong emphasis on having appropriate subject knowledge. Whilst there is strong support for the importance of professional development and the use of evidence to support classroom practice there is little acknowledgement of research or the encouragement of a questioning approach to current practice. There is a danger that this could result in the development of restricted professionals who find it difficult to adapt their practice to different conditions and circumstances and who merely replicate existing professional practice. However, supporters of this method of training would argue that a teacher who has been through this training programme will have a good understanding of the 'realities' of the classroom, be well placed to implement current policies without being burdened by too much theory and have a good subject knowledge which would enable them to become successful classroom practitioners.

We would argue that teachers have to be effective classroom practitioners and be able to maintain high standards. Working in the classroom alongside experienced teachers is an important part of any training programme. However, teachers should be made aware of a variety of approaches and be encouraged to question their own and others' practice. A collaborative approach between schools and HE would seem a logical way of ensuring this takes place and trainee teachers are encouraged to use research to improve their own classroom practice.

Conclusion

There has been an ongoing change in the role of the major stakeholders involved in teacher training. Recent policy has stressed the growing importance of schools and their teachers in all aspects of the process. HE staff have, at best, seen their role change and at worst they have been totally replaced by staff in school. This has had a considerable impact on individuals' working lives and also the institutions in which they work. The individual subject areas we identified in earlier chapters, such as educational philosophy or the sociology of education, have almost disappeared. There is much greater emphasis on practical issues based around classroom practice. A number of HE institutions have withdrawn from teacher training and this trend is likely to continue if government policy continues to favour school-based teacher training routes. However, there are still strong school and HE partnerships with good collaborative practice working in a number of areas and we will see some examples of this in later chapters.

Continuation of the present system will continue to lead to a variety of training routes being available with increasing numbers of providers and significant local variations in practice. Many more school staff are now involved in working with trainee teachers and this has created some additional pressures for schools. It has, however, provided significant professional development opportunities for a large number of teachers who now have the opportunity to work with trainee teachers. The process of marketisation and continuing reform has transformed the way in which teacher education is provided and the focus of the training process. There is a possibility that if current trends persist HE involvement in teacher education will be removed. It is interesting to note that we may be returning to an apprentice model which we discussed at the beginning of this book. The pressures brought about by rising pupil numbers and a shortage of entrants to the teaching profession may have a pragmatic impact on policy development. As Universities UK (2014: 1) pointed out, 'Universities across the UK are important hubs for their local area, training the people every community relies on, including ... 75,000 teachers'.

In the next series of chapters we will describe and consider how some of the policy changes have been implemented and how they impact on HE, schools and trainee teachers. The practical impact of government policies will be described by individuals who have been involved in the development and provision of a range of programmes. However, in Chapter 6 we consider how a number of other countries have developed their teacher education programmes and the training methods they have adopted to ensure a regular supply of high-quality teachers within some of the most successful education systems.

6
INTERNATIONAL PERSPECTIVES

> There is a widespread international consensus that, if modern societies are to flourish, if they are to strengthen their economic productivity, and if they are to ensure that all of their citizens lead satisfying personal lives, they need, through their educational systems, to cultivate the skills and capabilities of all, so that all can achieve their best potential. The same consensus affirms that the quality of teaching is the most crucial in-school factor in raising the level of pupils' achievement and furthering their educational progress.
> *(Minister for Employment and Learning, 2014)*

The above reference to the 'quality of teaching' is valuable because it identifies a central concern of this chapter, namely, the attempt to identify and understand the critical importance of teacher education in those education systems that have acquired the label of 'high-performing education systems' (HPSs). It is recognised that these systems have become 'reference societies' (Deng and Saravanan, 2015: 1), and it is accepted that all too frequently many policy makers across the globe look to such systems to find the 'quick fix' that will enable them to raise achievement levels in their societies, to enable them to compete successfully in the twenty-first century. There is a belief that we can learn lessons from one another, with the caveat that when looking at teacher education in high-performing systems, the dangers of accepting 'what works' without robust and legitimate evidence bases are acknowledged.

Indeed, recent education secretaries in England, such as Gove and Morgan, have followed the policy-borrowing trend and appear to have rushed to 'import' to England, for example, teachers of mathematics from Shanghai to teach in English schools. It should be noted that the activities of policy borrowing and policy tourism are not something new. In the nineteenth century English educators, such as Matthew Arnold, travelled overseas to report on schooling in Europe for the Royal Commission on Education of 1859 (Phillips and Schweisfurth, 2006).

There is what could be described as an unprecedented focus on teacher education, teacher quality and teacher performance as part of the 'policy-borrowing process'. A key issue highlighted by the Northern Ireland report (2014), is the role of teacher training as a critical factor to be taken into account by those countries wishing to improve the educational performance of their systems. How teachers are recruited, prepared and retained is an important topic in political, academic and public discourse about education in most countries. The evidence suggests that many policy makers are looking beyond their own systems to identify practices that they can learn from.

Inevitably, any discussions about 'policy borrowing' raise questions about the issues that arise when comparing international systems of education. Key issues relating to such comparisons include: the robustness of the evidence base; the validity and reliability of the methodologies of the various international survey results; and the rationale for the use of international league tables (Crossley and Sprague, 2012).

Previous chapters have described and commented on the development of, and approaches to, teacher training systems in England. This chapter builds on previous discussion and comments on the approaches to teacher training and continuing professional development and learning in five 'high-performing nations'. Finland, Hong Kong, Ontario, Shanghai, Singapore, and South Korea are included in the discussion, as these are currently recognised as being very successful in international comparisons of educational achievement.

The chapter identifies a number of key factors related to the literature on comparative educational systems and processes, which can be used to study issues associated with teacher education and continuing professional development. There is also some discussion of the different types of policy and practice that 'high-performing nations' have established, to shape the quality of their respective teaching work forces. Key features related to teacher education in the national picture in the six systems are explored, but the chapter does not claim to provide more than a 'snapshot' of practices in the education systems at a particular time (Furlong et al., 2009).

The key features that are briefly discussed are:

- system characteristics, including the centralisation and decentralisation of education policy;
- the status of teachers in society;
- the recruitment, selection and initial education of teachers;
- the role of teachers in curriculum and pedagogical issues;
- induction and support for newly qualified teachers;
- continuing professional development;
- the role of higher education institutions; and
- the influence of international testing and global rankings on policy makers.

A selection of high-performing systems nations was made on the basis of the recognition given to them in the literature for their consistency as high performers in international tests and in subsequent global rankings, such as the Programme for International Student Assessment (PISA) and Trends in International Mathematics and Science Study (TIMSS). For each system, a brief case study comments on its key features and also identifies other factors discussed in the literature which impact on the 'perceived' success of these systems. It is readily acknowledged that there have been, and are, very different policies and practices operating in these systems, which makes the rush to find the 'secrets' behind the success of these systems a formidable challenge.

The terms 'teacher education', 'initial teacher education' and 'teacher training' are commonly used in the literature. In this chapter, it is recognised that these terms refer to a phase in the processes in which teachers are prepared, inducted and developed as members of the teaching profession. The term 'teacher education' is used in this chapter and is used to highlight the different phases of initial teacher education, induction and continuing professional development.

Teacher education systems have been increasingly subject to international scrutiny and comparisons and assessed against each other in order to identify 'success criteria', which can be used to influence policy and practice in teacher education. For example, the Organisation for Economic Co-operation and Development (OECD) and the European Union have subjected teacher education policy and practice to increasing scrutiny and there is growing interest in international influences on education policy.

In each of the case studies, it is recognised that the ways in which teacher education is structured and the content of teacher education programmes are not unproblematic. Inevitably, there are political, social, economic and ideological pressures which affect these programmes. Indeed, there are often direct political pressures exerted over teacher education, dependent on the specific ideology of the government at the time. In a study of the role of research in international policy and practice in teacher education, Tatto (2013: 2), in a review of policy, practice and research in teacher education, writes: 'Nevertheless, current teacher education policy in countries such as England and the US, among others, continues to be influenced more by ideology, politics and tradition than by evidence of what works as shown by rigorous research'. This is an important point and will be discussed later in the chapter when comparisons are made between the teacher education systems of the different case-study nations.

Canada (Ontario)

Gambhir et al., in their study of themes and issues in initial teacher education in Canada, note that 'there has been increasing attention to, and debate about, the critical ingredients of a high quality initial teacher education (ITE) program, within the broader context of lifelong professional learning' (2008: 3). Although this statement was made some time ago, the key issue relating to the quality of initial teacher education has remained a major challenge for each of Canada's ten provinces and three territories, which have somewhat distinct systems of education. However, by most accounts, Canada's education system is a strong one and Canadian students score well on PISA, TIMSS and other international rankings of student achievement.

The prioritisation of education is evident when considering that government funding for the system is a relatively high percentage of GDP. At the same time, Canadians have historically expressed a high level of satisfaction with their teachers, and teachers are viewed as playing a critical role in student learning and in the implementation of the government's provincial policies (Natale et al., 2013). The fact that teaching has historically been a respected profession in Canada has influenced Canada's success in being consistently able to recruit high-quality students into teaching, with the majority drawn from the top 30 per cent of their college cohorts.

The focus for this section is Ontario. According to Hargreaves and Shirley (2012: 109), 'Among the international leaders of educational achievement, the Canadian province of Ontario is at the very pinnacle of attention. Ontario is one of Canada's highest scorers on PISA and therefore one of the top performers in the world.' Hargreaves and Shirley also suggest that Ontario has developed an education system that is worth exploring, despite the fact that there have been recent overhauls to the system to deal with a glut of trained teachers. Canada's system of education is highly decentralised, unlike other high-performing countries, and consequently, states like Ontario have had relative freedom to develop systems for teacher recruitment, selection and development that are unique to them.

Ontario has a tradition since early 2000 of a commitment to developing and supporting teachers and school leaders, in particular, within a framework of capacity building, where the emphasis is placed on recruiting qualified individuals, their preparation, induction, professional development and career development and retention. Ontario's reforms rested heavily on the confidence the government had in the quality of the province's teaching force. The following practices are significant in producing and developing the Ontario work force:

- initial preparation and induction programmes are strong;
- professional learning opportunities are widely available;
- teachers are encouraged and supported in using research-based strategies to investigate school improvement initiatives;
- there is a comprehensive mentoring system in place using a variety of different models;
- there is a highly developed performance-management system;
- there are research-based academic programmes of learning complemented with mentored field experiences in schools and the community; and
- there are distinct career 'tracks' which allow teachers to focus, for example, on mentoring or curriculum issues.

Many of these practices are discussed in the commentaries on the other case studies in this chapter because of their significance and impact in HPSs. These strategies serve to support the commitment to getting the 'right' people into teaching, and then preparing them well, by offering a wide range of opportunities for professional development and growth. Significantly, such initiatives are monitored and evaluated and then modified in the light of feedback and research evidence. In terms of teacher recruitment, Ontario requires a minimum three-year post-graduate secondary degree from an acceptable post-secondary institution and one year of teacher education before one can teach.

Recently, Ontario, in order to deal with a surfeit of teacher graduates, has introduced a two-year degree programme to better prepare trainee teachers. It has been suggested that this oversupply of teachers in Ontario reflects the attractiveness of teaching as a profession and the respect with which teaching is held in the province (NCEE, 2016a). In 2015, the provincial government made changes to teacher education in order to improve the preparation and training of all teachers and to reduce the number of enrolments on teacher training programmes.

Taillefer (cited in Herrup, 2011) has commented that: 'Good teacher development and ongoing development while you are a teacher, is one of the key components in making our education system successful, making sure that teachers are well-prepared to face the challenges is important'.

Darling-Hammond and Rothman report that continuous professional learning is also a significant element in the Ontario system. For example, teachers have 'six professional activity days every school year to work with each other on activities related to key state and local priorities' (2011: 12). At the same time, there are other capacity-building opportunities such as collaborative enquiry, learning communities and the use of new technologies to improve teaching and learning. The culture of professional learning is recognised as the key to 'developing, delivering, and sustaining improved knowledge, processes, and practices for educational improvement' (NCEE, 2016a: 10).

There is also a recognition of the importance of activities that promote professional learning in school-to-school networks, the latter of which are encouraged to engage in collaborative inquiry focused on enriching student learning. Professional development is highly valued and teachers have individual growth plans, which are developed from an individual teacher's self-evaluation against a set of teacher quality standards. At the same time, as professional learning has such a high profile, teachers can gain additional qualifications for their professional learning.

The culture of professional learning that has prevailed in Ontario since the major 2000 reforms enables capacity building and the development of strong partnerships between teachers, school leaders, district leaders and the government (NCEE, 2016a). The amount of support given to trainee teachers contributes to what is recognised as an extremely low attrition rate. Fullan (2012) notes that the Ontario approach, by focussing on teacher development, has also raised teacher accountability, while at the same time focussing significant reform efforts on investments in staffing and teacher development. The Ontario approaches have contributed to the fact that Ontario is an outstanding international performer in education and has achieved iconic success on international benchmarks (Hargreaves and Shirley, 2012: 130).

Finland

The excellent recent performance of Finnish learners in international assessments has aroused considerable world-wide interest and has encouraged people to inquire about the characteristics and atmosphere of Finnish schools and especially the working conditions, as well as the apparent enthusiastic, committed orientation of Finnish teachers. The general agreement is that high scores in international assessments and achievement tests are largely the result of the high quality of teachers and teacher education and development.

In the early 1970s, Finland recognised that its education system was underperforming and, therefore, widespread reforms were introduced, with particular emphasis placed on the selection and preparation of future high-quality teachers. Two key aspects of the reforms were the decisions to move teacher education to universities in 1971 and to introduce, in 1978, master's degree programmes for all teachers. It is clear that Finland was 'ahead of the game' with the latter initiative, and it has taken time for the leading systems to move in this direction (NCEE, 2016b).

Sahlberg succinctly describes the path that Finland has taken in the educational transformation of its system:

> The Finns have worked systematically over 35 years to make sure that competent professionals who can craft the best learning conditions for all students are in all schools, rather than thinking that standardised instruction and related testing can be brought in at the last minute to improve student learning and turn around failing schools.
>
> *(Sahlberg, 2009: 22)*

The reforms have focussed on a number of core principles and these include, as Laukkanen has noted, a 'pre-eminent emphasis on qualified teachers' (Laukkenen, 2008: 319). A central tenet of the reforms was that investment in teachers and in teacher education was essential. Policy makers recognised that they should seek to develop skilful teachers capable of acting autonomously and inter-dependently in their professional practice. Key stakeholders recognised that there should be a new culture of education characterised by trust between education authorities and schools, that there should be a priority given to local control, that professionalism should be promoted as a key aspect of teachers' work and that there should be opportunities for all stakeholders to practise with autonomy.

Since the 1990s, a central concern of teacher education developments in Finland has been to prepare teachers for a research-based profession. As has been noted, teachers are expected to hold master's degrees in both their content area and in education, and they are trained in both research methods and in pedagogic practice. The focus on highly intellectual and deeply clinical preparation is an outstanding aspect of the Finnish system. There are model schools, closely aligned to a local university, which help to develop and model innovative practices as well as foster research on learning and teaching. Finnish departments of teacher education have close relationships with teacher training schools and both have a high degree of autonomy.

Recruitment and selection into teacher education is very competitive from the pool of college graduates and only about 10 per cent of those who apply are admitted. In 2013, more than 8,000 people applied for 800 places for primary teaching positions, while at the University of Helsinki, there were 1,800 applicants for 120 places for trainee teachers. There has been a growth of 18 per cent in the number of applicants since 2010.

Musset (2010: 20), in her study of initial teacher education from a comparative perspective, observes that in the selection process in Finland: 'the entry into the initial teacher education programme is based on final secondary school results, as well as relevant work experience; followed by a second selection phase, made up of interviews and essays, as well as observed teaching lessons". It could be argued, then, that this strategic approach to initial teacher education increases the likelihood that student teachers will be suitable for the profession, highly motivated and will possess superior academic skills. Oates comments on the teacher training that is offered to trainee-teachers: 'only ten percent of applicants have been accepted for teacher training and these are selected on the basis of capability in developing – through the five to six years of research-intensive initial teacher training – high expertise in specialist subjects and in teaching approaches' (Oates, 2015: 4). A similar point is made by Hokka and Etalapelto (2013: 4) in a study of Finnish teacher education. They point out that all courses in Finnish teacher education have been purposely developed 'to train autonomous and reflective teachers capable of adopting a research-oriented attitude toward their work'.

In Finland, the training for prospective teachers is lengthy and rigorous and, as has been noted, it is based in universities – a contentious issue in many countries where the organisation and control of initial teacher education is contested, for example in England. There is extensive practice in schools for trainee teachers in Finland, and the training incorporates an extended project in educational research. As Hargreaves and Shirley note, this approach is recognised as one that is committed to: (Hargreaves and Shirley, 2012: 49).

It is interesting to note that in terms of career advancement, Finland does not have specific leadership roles for teachers; rather, teachers are provided with significant autonomy with respect to how they approach curriculum design and teaching. The high academic content of teacher education, and the focus on developing teachers who are able to resolve everyday teaching problems on the basis of theoretical knowledge, is recognised as a critical factor in teacher professionalism.

It is clear that Finland is one of the world's leaders in the academic performance of its secondary school students, a position it has held since 2000. In Finland there has been, over the years, commitment from all governments to educate all children in a system characterised by teaching excellence, and schools which are committed to collective responsibility for all children's educational success, working with and supporting a climate of trust between educators and the community.

In conclusion, key elements of the system in Finland, following Sahlberg (2010), can be summarised as follows: the Finnish teaching profession continues to be one that is revered; the focus on universities as the major player in teacher preparation and training is continually emphasised and the emphasis is on quality control as entry into the profession. As in other HPSs, teachers, at all stages in their careers, are considered as valued professionals who are capable, autonomous and independent and fully responsible for their work in the classroom.

China (Shanghai)

Shanghai first topped the global education league tables in 2009 and has remained a consistent performer since then. Understandably, the Shanghai achievements have engendered considerable interest in the strategies that Shanghai has put in place to achieve success. Obviously, Shanghai is not representative of all parts of China, but its importance and value to the whole country are evidenced by the fact that it is often given the privilege of experimenting with reforms before they are endorsed for other parts of the nation (OECD, 2010b). Shanghai is therefore an interesting example to examine in terms of identifying and understanding the strategies that have been established to initiate change, and to sustain improvement and progress in teacher education.

Teaching in Shanghai, it should be noted, is oversubscribed and teaching is a career that many qualified individuals want to enter and remain in.

Over 95 per cent of teachers have degrees from the two major teacher-preparation institutions (NCEE, 2016c), so there is coherence and confidence in the ways in which trainee teachers are prepared and developed. Some of the following initiatives relating to teacher education and development have been highlighted as factors in explaining Shanghai's high-quality achievements:

- Shanghai holds teachers in high regard and teaching is a high-status profession, and its system of valuing, preparing, supporting and recognising teachers is seen as a major contributor to the results that Shanghai has obtained in recent years (NCEE, 2016c).
- Expectations of teachers are extremely high. All new teachers are expected to complete 360 hours of continuing professional development in their own time in their first three years of teaching. It is not compulsory and is one third funded by the teacher, one third by the school and one third by the municipal authority. The 360 hours are organised at least in part around a master's degree provided by the universities.
- Over the years, teachers' threshold qualifications have been significantly elevated and today Shanghai requires all teachers to have a bachelor's degree in the subject they will teach – all teachers should have an undergraduate major in the subject they will teach (Tucker, 2014b).
- All primary schoolteachers must have a sub-degree diploma and all teachers in secondary schools are degree holders with professional certification. Many

teachers have master's degrees. Shanghai was the first district in China to require continuing professional development for teachers.
- In school, all teachers are part of teaching and research groups based around their subject and around the grade they are teaching. The groups meet for 90 minutes each week to discuss classroom teaching and jointly plan the next week's work. Class sizes are large and so the number of hours each teacher teaches is relatively low – up to 15 hours in secondary schools and up to 18 hours in primary schools.
- Shanghai's system of professional development is just one aspect of a system in which the improvement process is led by classroom teachers treated as true professionals. Teachers are taught research methods during their professional preparation and are expected to use those methods as they work in groups in their schools, to systematically improve teaching practices. Teachers work in an organisational environment which they are improving continuously.
- One feature that is fairly unique in the Shanghai system is the apprenticeship model, which is used to induct new teachers into the profession. The former are 'apprenticed' to master teachers and together, and often with other teachers from the same subject or grade area, have regular weekly meetings. Here, they collaborate in examining and trialling ways of improving knowledge, understanding and practice in key areas such as classroom questioning. The emphasis on mentoring and collaboration among teachers who work together to continually improve learning in the classrooms is at the heart of the matter. In this approach, teachers recognise that they are accountable to one another for their performances.
- At the same time, new teachers are observed frequently and receive a lot of feedback and help on lesson planning and teaching styles. A key aim is to ensure that new teachers are supported in improving their mastery in a very disciplined way. The teacher development system that was built over this period reflects not only years of careful and incremental reform, but also the design of a self-reinforcing system that continually improves (Zhang et al., 2016: 18).

Teachers, once they join the teaching force, are expected to continue to improve and refine their practice throughout their careers. The *jiaoyanzu*, or 'teacher research group', is an important and unique form of professional learning in schools in China, and hence in Shanghai. Activities such as research, peer observation, lesson evaluation, visits to other schools and taking feedback from students and colleagues are used alongside 'lesson preparation groups' to provide ongoing professional learning opportunities for teachers. The system of professional development for teachers is similar to those in other East Asian systems. The professional development system is one important strategy for achieving high standards in individual schools and greater consistency across schools throughout the whole system.

A major strength of teacher education and training in Shanghai, according to a recent NCEE (2016c) report, is that it occupies a unique status within Chinese education policy. It is able to develop its own policies based on national Ministry of Education guidelines and is used as a test-bed for innovations and for rolling out new policies.

Singapore

Since self-government in 1959, education has been both the key source of competitive strength and a necessity for the economic growth and social viability of Singapore (Tan et al., 2007). Singapore is frequently ranked among the top performers in educational attainment, as measured by the OECD's PISA assessment regime. Tan (2015:1), in a review of education in Singapore, states that: 'Singapore's education system has been much lauded for its achievements in delivering quality schooling to its citizens. It consistently tops international educational rankings, produces students that win international competitions, and churns out graduates that are among the most desired in the world'.

Education in Singapore has been described as: 'a highly functioning system which has undergone and continues to undergo important structure, resources and process change' (Tatto, 2013: 8). It is clear that the Singapore government, through the Ministry of Education, is able to exercise centralised control over the school curriculum and, importantly, over teacher education. There are very close ties between the Ministry of Education and the National Institute of Education, which is a significant factor in ensuring that change initiatives are effective 'on the ground'.

A key strength of the Singaporean system has been the commitment to a process of continuous review, refinement and evaluation of its education policies and practices, as a means of continuous improvement over the years. As Hogan (2014) has noted, over time, Singapore has developed a powerful set of institutional arrangements that shape its instructional regime. Singapore has developed an education system which is centralised (despite significant decentralisation of authority in recent years), integrated, coherent and well funded. It is also relatively flexible and expert-led.

Unsurprisingly, it has been noted that Singapore: 'aggressively pursued a policy of advancing education and other arenas by systematically benchmarking the world's best performance and creating a world-class education system based on what it had learned through their benchmarking' (Brown-Martin, 2014: 67). Using knowledge gained from this commitment to learn from others and the desire for improvement, the Ministry of Education has been prepared to implement, since the mid-1990s, paradigm shifts in the system, so that Singapore would be fully prepared to meet the needs of the twenty-first century (Sharpe and Gopinathan, 2002). For example, Singapore introduced a Teacher Education Model for the 21st Century in 2009, recognising that its twenty-first-century learners would need twenty-first-century teachers, with twenty-first-century literacies themselves, and the ability to create the appropriate learning environments that would allow students to develop the required skills and knowledge for the twenty-first century (Stewart 2010/11).

There has been a continued recognition of the value and importance of an appropriately qualified and versatile teaching force to meet the demands of the rapidly changing environment. Investment in high-quality teacher education has led to the situation where Singapore is often used as a model for teacher education reformers (DEL, 2014: 74). High-quality education is supported through a comprehensive system for selecting, training, developing and rewarding teachers.

Prospective teachers are selected from the top third of secondary school students and standards for selection are very high. Outstanding academic and non-academic qualifications are essential for entry to teacher training programmes, as well as a commitment to the profession and to serving the nation's diverse needs (Ho, 2010). The selection process for trainee teachers is rigorous and is managed as a state-wide process, involving the Ministry of Education and the National Institute of Education.

Singapore reviewed and altered its teacher education programmes in 2001, in order to ensure that there was a heavy focus on developing teachers' pedagogical skills as well as content knowledge. This initiative is helping Singapore to move towards graduate-level training for its trainee teachers.

A meritocratic approach governs the development and promotion of teachers: top-performing teachers are given leadership responsibilities and there is a 'revolving door' between the Ministry of Education, schools and school administration. The development of the Academy of Singapore Teachers in 2010, has provided opportunities for teacher-led professional learning. The academy collaborates with the Ministry of Education and National Institute of Education to embed professional learning within schools.

After graduation, all teachers participate in a generous system of professional development, which reflects the philosophy that the key to developing outstanding teachers is the provision of key incentives and appropriate opportunities to develop as professionals. New teachers are entitled to 100 hours of professional development every year. Continuing professional development provided by the National Institute of Education focusses on subject matter and pedagogical knowledge and leads to higher degrees. Professional development is primarily school-based, led by professional development staff, whose responsibility is to identify issues in the school that need improvement.

Teachers are appraised Annually, and their appraisal assesses their contribution to the academic and character development of their students, their corroborations with parents and the community, and their contribution to colleagues and the school as a whole. This appraisal helps the teacher to identify areas of growth that inform the basis of personal professional development plans. To support ongoing professional development, Singapore champions mentoring as a highly valued feature of all schools. The Structured School Mentoring Program is a required duty of teacher leaders, who are given prime responsibility for supporting and mentoring new teachers.

In a review of four HPSs, Hargreaves and Shirley (2012: 89) refer to an OECD report (2010b) which highlights the Singaporean policy strengths. These include: 'Close links between policy implementers, researchers and educators; commitment to continuous improvement and constant comparison with and learning from best practice around the world; and effective human resource management in the selection, development, and retention of teachers and leaders' (Hargreaves and Shirley, 2012: 89–90).

Hogan (2014) has argued that Singapore is strongly committed to capacity building at all levels of the system and, in addition, parents, students, teachers and policy-makers share a highly positive, but rigorously instrumentalist, view of the value of education at the individual level. The challenge now is focussed on how this successful system can be sustained into the twenty-first century.

South Korea

Attention has focussed on the South Korean education system because its students have consistently scored highly on international tests, for example the PISA tests. Inevitably, there has been interest in teacher selection, recruitment and training and the relationship between these factors and success in the international testing regime. Morris points out that: Morris has suggested that education has been strongly harnessed to nation-building and instilling a strong sense of national identity (2013). At the same time, in the post-war period there have been several major reforms of the system and, in particular, in teacher education. South Korea has placed a strong emphasis on education, which is one reason why their country has advanced so quickly in the last half century.

Teaching is a relatively sought-after occupation and the teaching profession has achieved a high social status. Consequently, those who aspire to become teachers are usually highly qualified and highly motivated (Ingersoll, 2007). Teaching continues to be a popular career choice among young people, due to a combination of its high social status, job stability and high remuneration. The teaching profession is traditionally respected in Korean society and the social status and salary levels are higher than in many other countries. Teachers are selected from the top 5 per cent of graduate students in Korean education (Barber and Mourshed, 2007). The proportion of all South Korean teachers that are fully certified and hold bachelor's degrees is among the highest in the world.

The system of teacher education is highly regulated at the elementary level, with the country's 11 teachers' colleges being relatively selective. However, at the secondary level there are multiple pathways to certification, including attendance at a comprehensive university, with selection occurring at the hiring phase. This raises questions about the quality of some of the secondary courses and the South Korean government has tried to address these issues by improving the accreditation system for teacher education programmes, revising the curriculum and improving the relationship between teachers' colleges and universities. There have been regular shortages of elementary teachers and it has been estimated that on occasions, only 30 per cent of secondary candidates can find jobs.

After their fourth year of teaching, South Korean teachers are required to take 90 hours of professional development courses every three years. Also, after three years of teaching, teachers are eligible to enrol in a five-week (180-hour) professional development programme approved by the government, to obtain an advanced certificate which provides an increase in salary and eligibility for promotion (Darling-Hammond et al., 2010: 5). There is good provision for ongoing professional development. Upon successful completion, they become 'full' teachers, with a better chance for later promotion to headteacher and a small salary increase. Professional development is managed at the state and/or school district level.

South Korea is currently institutionalising a master teacher system, piloted in 2008. Master teachers must have 10–15 years of experience. They remain in a teaching role, but are expected to share their expertise with less experienced teachers as well and develop curriculum, instructional practices and evaluation systems.

It has to be pointed out that the Ministry of Education is the central administrative authority that develops teacher education policies, to ensure a flexible supply of teachers in the context of the prevailing needs and national demands. A highly centralised system is able to ensure equality and quality across the nation in relation to the recruitment and deployment of high-quality teachers. In South Korea, reforms to the evaluation and development of teacher education continue to improve the quality of initial teacher training.

Conclusion

This chapter concludes with comments about a range of factors that have been identified as influencing the success of high-performing systems. It is, however, recognised that there are contested views about these factors, which are rooted in different views about teaching and schooling in local and national cultures (Menter et al., 2010). The key factors which have informed discussion in the sections on individual nations are as follows.

Centralisation and decentralisation of educational systems and policy

In the systems reviewed, it is clear that the Ministry of Education or its equivalent body usually exercises a great degree of control over the system by: being selective about entry requirements to teacher education programmes; controlling student supply; controlling the qualification and accreditation system; and monitoring closely the content, the quality and the outcomes of education programmes. In Singapore, for example, the ministry directly oversees teacher recruitment and training through the National Institute of Education.

System characteristics

In this review of successful systems, specific characteristics have emerged that are shared by these systems, and these include a focus on: acceptance that it is the system that is responsible for student success, not just the student, the teacher or the parent; a high degree of coherence in curriculum matters; teaching and learning; high academic standards; and a belief in equity (Deng and Saravanan, 2015).

The status of teachers in society

In countries where the teaching profession is highly valued in society, such as Finland, Singapore and South Korea, students seem to learn more effectively

(Burns and Darling-Hammond, 2014). Moreover, teachers' positive sense of their status is closely linked to other aspects of quality education, including continuing professional development, engagement in research, collaboration and exchange with other teachers and involvement in decision making (Symeonidus, 2015: 14, citing Hargreaves and Flutter, 2013).

According to Hargreaves and Flutter (2013), several factors influencing the status of teachers are linked to political and policy changes. In many nations, there has been a growing emphasis on accountability policies, often at the expense of teachers' autonomy, and teachers increasingly feel under pressure. Several nations tend to introduce school inspection systems, publish league tables of school performance and adopt measures aimed at evaluating and raising standards. Social trends also influence the status of teachers, as can be seen in countries where the status remains high because parents and communities value teachers for their contribution to their children's development and future. There are also national contexts, where the public perception of teachers' status exceeds teachers' own perception of their status, for example in Belgium's Flanders, where teachers have steadily been accorded higher esteem by society over the last 40 years (Verhoeven et al., as cited in Hargreaves and Flutter, 2013: 12).

It is apparent that most high-performing systems prioritise the establishment of career paths that are rewarding and sustainable. There are emphases, as Darling-Hammond (2010) notes, on horizontal promotion systems that allow teachers to maintain their contributions to improving teaching and learning in the classroom, rather than through taking on management responsibilities.

Teacher education: recruitment, selection and induction

In the main, high-performing systems have rigorous selection systems that control entry into the teaching profession and they recruit teachers from the top of the pool of talented applicants who apply for entry to the profession. Thus, systems such as Finland, South Korea and Singapore attract all of their teachers from the top third of their respective academic cohorts. There are differences in policy details between and within systems as to how teachers are selected, but the outcomes are very similar; each system appears to recruit from cohorts of high-calibre, academically skilled and committed applicants, who then benefit from quality initial teacher education. What appears to be universal in all these countries is that teachers generally come from the top of their graduation cohort and that the teaching profession is conferred with high status and often high pay. Many countries set attracting the 'best and the brightest' into teaching as a national priority.

It is also worth noting that in some systems, for example in Singapore, career paths are defined, well remunerated and matched to teacher interests. Teachers may choose between master teacher, curriculum developer or school leader positions (OECD, 2010b). The NCEE policy brief, 'Recruiting and Selecting Excellent Teachers' (2016d: 9), notes that: 'teacher candidates in high-performing systems are expected to demonstrate a range of competencies and dispositions, that are surfaced in selection processes, that extend beyond transcripts and grades'. I have added a colon and inverted commas for a direct quotation.

The role of teachers in curriculum and pedagogical issues

High-quality systems are characterised by collaborative work cultures that promote teamwork and cooperation among their teaching staff. For instance, in Shanghai there is an emphasis on formalised systems of teamwork, in which teachers create public lessons based on action research which they share with their colleagues for feedback and refinement in subject-based 'teaching study groups' (Schleicher, 2012). In most systems, trainee teachers and newly appointed teachers are provided with opportunities to carry out high-level research to inform practice. At the same time, there is an emphasis on continuous training in both subject content and pedagogy, with opportunities for staff to plan and evaluate teaching with one another. Most systems invest in support for regular and systematic opportunities to enhance the quality of continuing professional development

Continuing professional development

High-performing systems are characterised by opportunities for staff to engage in sustained professional development in collaborative professional communities with support from expert mentors and coaches. In Ontario and in Finland, there is a commitment to engage all teachers in embedded systems of teacher collaboration, action research and sharing of practice.

There is therefore, in these systems, according to Barber and Moushed (2007), space and time for more professional collaboration, planning and careful monitoring of student achievement, with the use of research and enquiry as a way to develop an informed, reflective teaching profession

The role of higher education institutions in teacher education

In the majority of the case-study examples, higher education institutions have responsibility for the provision and delivery of teacher training programmes. It is unusual for there to be mainly school-based systems. One exception is England, which has been discussed in Chapter 5, where a school-based policy towards teacher education has been championed by various governments. This is not to say, however, that English higher education institutions do not continue to play an important role in teacher education.

In contrast to the system in England, Finland, South Korea and Singapore, for example, place universities at the heart of their teacher education provision. As has been stated in previous sections, in Finland, recruitment to the teaching profession is highly selective and teachers are required to hold a master's degree. At the same time, trainee teachers experience training which is research-based, and there is a strong emphasis on pedagogical content knowledge. Teacher education in South

Korea takes place at universities or dedicated teachers' colleges, while in Singapore the National Institute of Education is the only teacher training institution.

The role and value of international testing

The evidence from international surveys such as PISA and TIMSS indicates that countries with improved performance and more equitable systems have introduced more stringent requirements for teaching qualifications, incentives to attract high achievers into teaching, effective professional development and career development opportunities (European Commission, 2014).

Concluding comments

Teacher quality is linked to, and/or dependent on, an effective and appropriate initial teacher education (McKinsey & Co., 2007; Freedman et al., 2008). Therefore, policy-makers and system leaders have increasingly looked at how appropriate and effective their own systems are and, in order to develop high-quality teachers, have engaged in reform and change with regards to their teacher education systems.

There are a number of common factors, essential for all nations, which serve to help shape the status of the teaching profession and play a crucial role in delivering quality and ensuring equity in education. Moyle (2015: 8), in a discussion of teacher education in high-performing systems based on a review of the literature, identifies the following issues which are related to policies and practices and which are 'aligned and interconnected, funded and implemented':

- public investment in education;
- creating identifiable career paths in teaching;
- attracting high-quality applicants;
- employing effective quality-assurance policies and procedures; and
- working in partnership with schools to train teachers.

Discussions about how to improve the education system must take into account the evidence of the high-performing systems. It is difficult to make substantial long-term improvement to a system without focussing on raising the quality of people who enter the teaching profession and attracting people into teaching who choose teaching as the preferred career. There are, therefore, strong processes for selecting and training teachers, paying good starting salaries and carefully managing the status of the teaching profession. The top-performing systems demonstrate that the quality of an education system depends ultimately on the quality of its teachers.

It has to be acknowledged that context, culture, politics and systems of government are critical factors in achieving real improvement. Thus, it is necessary to recognise that different systems have distinct and unique histories, cultural factors and institutional characteristics that inform how their education systems perform, and it is impossible to suggest that, despite the current preoccupation with 'policy borrowing' and 'policy tourism', these systems can be 'reproduced' to transform teacher education in other countries.

Wilkins (2014: 1), in his discussion of school leadership in a global context, comments that: 'The global changes affecting school systems are creating conditions of dynamism, complexity and uncertainty'. These issues are evident in the ways in which complex education systems attempt to adapt to the changing needs of their societies and their economies. The HPSs referred to in this chapter provide evidence that an emphasis on recruitment, development, retention and advancement of teachers is essential to the economic, political and social wellbeing of the case-study nations. The chapter has identified some of the key features of high-performing systems and emphasises that initial teacher education is ideally positioned to play a significant and strategic role in informing and enacting effective policy changes.

7

MODELS OF PROVISION

higher education

As we have argued earlier, the involvement of higher education (HE) in the training of teachers in England has been long standing and in this chapter we will discuss, from the perspective of those involved, the form and substance of this process. The role and amount of HE engagement in the training of teachers has been in decline as a result of the encouragement by successive governments of different providers to enter the market and the subsequent rise of alternative training routes (Murray and Mutton, 2016). The development of alternative routes into teaching has reduced the extent and altered the nature of the work carried out by HE institutions (Junemann and Ball, 2013; Ellis et al., 2015). However, it is important to recognise the remaining large-scale involvement of HE providers, and we provide some accounts of this activity from the perspective of the staff and trainee teachers who participate in this process.

Case study 1: primary PGCE trainer

Our first example is provided by Jenny Bosworth, head of the Primary PGCE at the University of Leicester. The following illustrates the range of programmes HE institutions are involved in and the nature of the activity.

The Primary PGCE at the University of Leicester has been well established for over 60 years and during its most recent Ofsted inspection in 2015, it was graded as 'Outstanding'. Although the course has seen a decline in numbers over the last few years, reflecting a national trend, there were 85 students undertaking the course during the academic year 2017/18. These numbers include several different routes into teaching. The Lower Primary course (ages 3–7) the Primary course (ages 5–11) and the Primary with Maths course (5–11) cover our 'university-led' routes. Our Primary with Maths course gives students with an interest in mathematics the chance to develop their knowledge and understanding through extra maths-based sessions and tasks to carry out in school. An important part of initial teacher education is preparation of the students for their continuing professional development. The focus of the Primary with Maths course is to develop some of the skills necessary to take on maths leadership or coordination within a school relatively early in their careers.

All routes involved with the Primary PGCE are master's-level courses. If students successfully complete, they will be recommended for qualified teacher status (QTS) as well as achieving 60 master's credits. The majority of our students follow the 'university-led' route. The university arranges their three contrasting placements and delivers the taught elements of the course. The university also works with several School Direct (SD) providers. At the University of Leicester, students on the SD route follow the same pattern of placements, however, this may take place across two different contrasting schools, as arranged by the SD provider. Most of our SD providers also choose to buy into the whole of the taught course. They can choose to deliver one or more of the strands of the course themselves.

The 'strands' of the Primary PGCE comprise the university-based taught elements of the course. These include maths, English, science, professional, broader curriculum and academic. The various strands contain a variety of different contributors, both from inside and outside of the university, as well as modelling different teaching strategies, methods and styles. They are taught in an interactive, practical way which incorporates some of the techniques they might use in the classroom. The pedagogical nature of teaching is the main focus of the professional strand and is timetabled to allow preparation for, and reflection on, the three teaching placements. Within these sessions, the students discuss their experiences with each other and are able to support and learn from the perspectives of their peers. This is particularly helpful when thinking about the different year groups which students may find themselves in throughout the year and the challenges they might face in adapting their practice. It also models the importance of talk for learning and allows them to see the benefit of using this technique with children in school.

Much of the teaching in initial teacher education adopts this multi-layered approach to teaching: the specific subject knowledge, pedagogical knowledge and knowledge of the National Curriculum. Each session within the strands will contain elements of all these aspects of teaching, with an expectation on the students to take responsibility for the advancement of their own subject knowledge. A crucial skill in teaching is awareness of your own subject knowledge, but ultimately being able to break it down and make it accessible to the children, at whatever age and stage they are working at.

Within the academic strand falls the 'specialism' component, where students can select a specialist subject. These typically include English, maths, science, early years and inclusion. This forms the basis for one of the two master's-level assignments, the first being a case study based on children's learning carried out during their first teaching placement.

The University of Leicester also works with several School-Centred Initial Teacher Training providers, who attend all academic sessions alongside the university-led and SD students. Within this strand they develop their knowledge of research methodology, educational theories and classroom-based research.

The current government requirement is that students are given the opportunity to spend at least 120 days in school during their training year. The University of Leicester Primary PGCE placements comprise a two-week preliminary placement at the beginning of September, before the taught course begins. This is designed to allow the students to see the organisation and planning that a teacher must do to ensure that their class settles well into the first few weeks of term.

A six-week placement in the autumn term follows an initial period of time in university. For the majority of students, this is a paired teaching placement. This allows them to support and learn from each other, during what can be a daunting first experience of teaching. There is then a six-week placement in the spring term and an eight-week placement in the summer term.

All elements of the course are assessed against the Teachers' Standards (DfE Research Report, 2012), including Part 2. The three placements are scaffolded in such a way that students build up to teaching 80 per cent of the timetable and can show consistent, sustained and independent teaching to a high standard.

Mentors and tutors are both involved in the assessment of the students against the Teachers' Standards. Mentors are usually the class teacher based in the class where the student is placed, although this is not always the case. They are invited to attend a full day's training on the principles and practicalities of mentoring before each placement. For SD students, the SD coordinator is also part of the assessment process.

During our recent Ofsted report, a number of strengths were identified. One which we have worked particularly hard to manage and maintain, and was consequently recognised as a strength, is the relationship we have with our partnership schools. Headteachers and other colleagues are involved in the planning and delivery of our course as well as supporting us in the recruitment and selection of prospective candidates. Our selection process was identified as being 'rigorous and effective' in the 2015 Ofsted report. This then translates into high employability figures, with our students being 'highly prized' by local headteachers.

As anyone who has completed a teacher training course can testify, it is a challenging time. Especially during a one-year, post-graduate course, where time is limited to learn and understand the complexities of teaching. Therefore, we prioritise the support we give our students throughout the year. Students are allocated a progress tutor, who monitors progress and collates information about the student throughout the year. Guidance and advice is offered in the form of regular tutorials, but students are encouraged to contact their progress tutor throughout the course, if needed. One of the roles of the progress tutor is to read and, where necessary, respond to the students' weekly reflection. This document is uploaded at the end of every week of the course and offers an insight into how the students are feeling, what they may be struggling with and, crucially, what is the impact on their future practice. Ultimately, teaching is about reflecting, evaluating and responding, and through this weekly tool we find that the students develop their skill of reflection until it is an instinctive part of their practice.

Inevitably, there are challenges. In a profession which is governed by an ever changing landscape of political agendas, national priorities and local requirements, the course must adapt and evolve around current perspectives. Our partnership management group is comprised of local headteachers and senior leaders who meet three times a year to identify, discuss and ultimately ratify changes or decisions made about the course. This overview of the content of the PGCE is therefore steeped in current educational priorities. This allows us the confidence of knowing that we are providing schools with newly qualified teachers (NQTs) who have been trained with their needs in mind and whose educational philosophies have developed through the input of our partner schools.

Our course is guided and strengthened through the input of partnership schools and this means that, in return, we are able to produce NQTs who will have been taught with a shared philosophy of reflective practice, helping learners reach their full potential and becoming part of a whole-school community.

The Teachers' Standards provide a comprehensive framework with which to assess students in their progress. The Standards Evidence descriptors further outline the skills and knowledge that a teacher needs to demonstrate in order to be assessed at the highest level throughout their training and beyond.

While all standards carry equal importance in their weighting, pupil progress is at the heart of every educational agenda. One of the challenges of initial teacher education is developing the skills of evaluation and reflection in students so that they assess their own practice in terms of what the children have learnt, as opposed to what they have taught. The shift in perspective from their actions to the impact that their actions have had on the children's learning is a turning point in their development as teachers.

The development of our course, based on feedback from Ofsted, external examiners and our school partners, now means that the focus of our assessments are largely around pupil progress. Documentation, training and directed tasks are designed with this in mind, in order to facilitate that shift in perspective which means that students respond effectively to the needs of the children at an earlier stage in their training.

Of course, we are constantly seeking to improve our course and have identified some areas on which we need to focus. Ensuring that assessment of students' understanding of pupil progress is rigorous and consistent is an area which is under constant review. Assessment, differentiation, responding to the needs of your learners and becoming familiar and fluent in mastery of all subjects are aspects of teaching which some experienced teachers would still find a challenge. These are complex, multi-faceted skills which require an in-depth knowledge of the learners. Quite a tall order during a six-week teaching placement, but nevertheless an expectation of teachers, regardless of experience or context.

Our year-on-year data show consistently high grades awarded to students at the end of their PGCE year. However, we identified that our male students were not always achieving as high grades as their female counterparts, or were not completing in the same time frame. The number of male students on the course was approximately 20 per cent, a figure which reflects the national average of male Primary teachers, both training and in post. Having carried out extensive research into some of the reasons why male students were not always as successful as our female students, we made some significant changes and additions to the course. The findings included the different expectations which were placed on male students, such as being automatically good at behaviour management, getting a job due to their gender and being expected to be a role model for particular children. Some of the changes we consequently made included ensuring that all male students had at least one male mentor and visiting tutor during the course, and the addition of a male-only support club, anecdotally referred to as 'Man Club'. This was a chance for the male students to discuss with an experienced male tutor some of the issues which they faced when going into school, which may not have applied to all students. A male NQT was also asked to attend one of the meetings to provide advice and support.

We have found that these measures, as well as being open with both students and partnership school colleagues about the issues that male students might face, has made a difference in closing the gap between the male and female student grades as well as opening up a useful dialogue with colleagues in other institutes where they have experienced similar challenges.

Further challenges which face any provider of initial teacher education may include the variety and complexity of the different routes into teaching. Trying to navigate around the information regarding the options available can be time consuming and result in any potential candidates feeling confused about where to start. Experience, background, current employment, financial situation and context can also be factors to be taken into consideration. It also means that each provider finds themselves in competition for an already declining pool of candidates. Ultimately, to ensure the best chance of success, candidates must choose a route which suits their circumstances and learning style best.

So, to the future. As previously mentioned, initial teacher training (ITT) sits in a constantly changing landscape, but the focus must always be the children who will be influenced by this landscape. Mental health and wellbeing of both teachers and children is high on the agenda for teachers and teacher educators alike. Retention of teachers is a national issue and one which, when unpicked, reveals a worrying trend of mental health implications for teachers. As this has been brought to our attention, not just through national media but from our partnership schools, it has now become part of the course which we are continuing to monitor and develop.

This has also led to an evaluation of the structure of our course, in terms of placements and taught timetable. While we want to provide students with a realistic idea of the workload and expectations of the profession that they are preparing to enter, we also want to maintain a manageable balance so that they do not simply exist in 'survival' mode as a student teacher. We want to develop students who are open-minded and able to see the wood for the trees. To have the ability to ask relevant questions and reflect on the answers as well as their own practice.

This will mean that they continue to develop as effective practitioners long after their PGCE year is completed.

Case study 1: primary PGCE trainee

A trainee perspective of the PGCE course at the University of Leicester is provided by Lauren Mintey, who completed the course in 2016/17.

Upon beginning the PGCE course, I was under no illusion as to how challenging the year ahead would be. After all, everyone is quick to tell you that the PGCE will be 'the hardest year of your life'. And it was. However, it was also one of the best, most rewarding and exciting years of my life, too.

My time on the PGCE was split between university-based taught sessions and gaining practical experience through three main teaching placements. Having recently graduated from my undergraduate degree, I expected the university-based elements of the course to involve sitting in lectures, making notes and reading books. I couldn't have been more wrong. The sessions were active, new ideas were thrown at us left, right and centre, and I was challenged to think about things in ways I had never thought of before. Every evening I would go home, my mind bustling with new information. I realised that for the first time in a long time, I felt genuinely interested and passionate about what I was studying. Not only that, but I can't quite believe just how much I learnt throughout the year.

My first placement was paired, meaning that I had another student teacher in the class to share that very first teaching experience with. On the first day of that placement, we led a circle time activity. All I remember was the other trainee and I looking helplessly at each other, unsure whether to laugh or cry at the chaos unfolding in front of us. We had an 'engaging hook'. We were shaking the tambourine as an 'attention grabber'. We had planned our timings to the minute, ensuring we maintained good 'pace'. We were doing everything we had been told to, but nothing seemed to work. At the time, I seriously questioned whether I'd ever be able to control a class of 30 children by myself. The next day, my time leading the class involved reading a story and all I remember was just how nervous I felt. Had I picked a good story? Does my voice sound silly? Was I asking appropriate questions? What does my mentor think of me? At the time I felt like a fish out of water; nervous and lacking confidence. Now I look back on these moments and not only laugh about them, but use them as a benchmark for just how much I developed as a teacher and as a person over the course of the PGCE year.

My second placement was definitely the most fun. By this point, I had developed a general confidence in the classroom, but the pressure of qualifying and becoming a 'real teacher' wasn't yet looming. I was placed at the same school as three other trainees, all of whom I still regularly meet with now. Together, we set up a lunchtime club, ran singing assemblies and supported each other daily with ideas and motivation. This placement proved to me that the support of your peers cannot be underestimated on a course like the PGCE, not only when you feel as though you may be struggling, but also in keeping things light-hearted and in maintaining that all important sense of wellbeing.

As with everything, with the highs also came a few lows. During this placement, I had what I would refer to as my 'worst' lesson observation. Don't get me wrong, it wasn't terrible. The children were well behaved and they all made progress with their learning. The word used to describe the lesson was 'flat'. It wasn't bad, it was just 'flat'. Flat. In that moment, I'd have rather the children behaved like animals and learnt nothing. I definitely took the feedback more personally than I should have and I'd be lying if I said that lesson didn't knock my confidence for a good few weeks. But, this is where that infamous word, 'reflection', came in. In the moment, a less than brilliant lesson could very easily make you feel like a bad teacher, but looking back, those were undoubtedly the lessons where I learnt most about effective teaching.

In my final placement, I vividly remember the time flying and panicking that in a matter of weeks I would be a qualified teacher. I knew that these upcoming observations would be the most important and my next stop would be a class of my own, with no one to check my lesson plans, no one to step in when I needed them and no one to tell me what to do. However, I think it was this pressure that spurred me on. It was during this placement that everything seemed to click and I finally began to feel like a 'proper' teacher and a valuable member of the team. Planning lessons was becoming easier, I felt more confident that children were making progress and I was effectively managing the behaviour of a class of post-SATs Year 6 children. A far cry from that first circle time!

One of the greatest challenges of the PGCE was, of course, the workload, and this seemed to intensify during the final placement. Lesson plans, evaluations, reflections, assessment-tracking grids, assignments, reflections, action plans, reports, teacher standards' evidence and yes, more reflections. Sometimes, when filling in these forms in the early hours of the morning or on a Saturday night, it was easy to resent their very existence, but they really were essential in helping to guide our development and, looking back now, I know that I wouldn't have learnt half as much without them.

Throughout the highs and the lows, one thing remained constant: the children. Throughout the madness of the training year it was sometimes easy to forget that they were the reason we were all there. Their one liners, their inquisitive minds, their laughter, their eagerness and excitement. They were often the ones to keep me sane when the workload seemed unmanageable, or an observation was looming. So yes, the PGCE is undoubtedly a tough year. Would I want to do it again? Absolutely. After all, where else would I be able to meet such like-minded people, be supported by experts in their field, get to experience the diversity of a number of schools, experiment and try new ideas, carry out my own research project and make lifelong friends along the way?

Case study 2: secondary PGCE trainer

A secondary PGCE perspective is provided by Kate Mawson, a senior teaching fellow in the Centre for Teacher Education at the University of Warwick.

Teacher education has existed on our site at Warwick since 1948. Through numerous name changes and iterations, we now exist as the Centre for Teaching Education and have an outstanding rating from OFSTED in both primary and secondary post-graduate teacher education. Our course centres on the effective consumption of research by trainee teachers, alongside reflective practice and practical classroom support. We offer a course where trainees can gain 90 CAT points towards our MA in Professional Education.

There are many routes into gaining recommendation for QTS: School-Centred Initial Teacher Training; SD salaried and trainee; QTS-only courses; the assessment-only route; Teach First's two-year programme; the less available three- or four-year Bachelor of Education, which still exists in some institutions, and of course the one-year PGCE.

We have been a popular course choice for many years and even in the current climate of recruitment difficulties, we are projecting that we will recruit 240 trainees in 2018/19 onto the secondary PGCE course (Table 7.1).

At Warwick, we offer PGCE for Core and SD places, that is to say, trainees who applied to and were interviewed by the university are Core, and trainees who applied to and were interviewed by schools are SD. There are a few differences to the requirement of each type of training, for instance SD trainees only require training in the 11–16 age group, whereas Core trainees require 11–18 experience in their training year. Both groups of trainees, however, gain the same recommendation for QTS and 90 CAT points on successful completion of the course.

We develop our course in partnership with many of our schools. There is a common structure for both PGCE SD and PGCE Core trainees, with the only difference being that SD trainees spend time with their lead alliance school. They receive four days of bespoke training created in schools, whilst the PGCE Core trainees return to university on these days for bespoke training and opportunities, such as mock interviews with school heads. SD trainees begin their training year with fuller timetables than Core trainees and some may receive a salary if they are experienced in the classroom setting; apart from this, the calendar year looks the same for all trainees.

Differently to a number of other courses, we begin our initial induction in the school summer holiday, which allows trainees to be ready to go into schools from the beginning of term. This receives a warm welcome from our school partners and trainees alike. Trainees then spend one day a week at university and the other four out in schools. We structure our course in this way so that issues discussed at university can be developed in schools, and issues arising in schools can contribute to the university programme. We are responsive to both our trainees and the schools' needs and the programme has an element of flexibility planned into it, so that we can react to changes in the education landscape as they occur. The course,

TABLE 7.1 PGCE applications and student numbers

Phase	Route	2018/19 applications	Percentage conversion application to accepted offer	2018/19 accepted offers	2017/18 applications	Percentage conversion application to accepted offer	2017/18 accepted offers	2016/17 applications	Percentage conversion application to accepted offer	2016/17 accepted offers
Secondary	Core	325	18	60	245	25	61	192	21	41
Secondary	SD	411	24	99	555	17	93	568	19	107
Secondary	All routes	736	22	159	800	19	154	760	19	148

however, is structured enough so that schools and trainees have the yearly calendar of topics when they start in August, discussed with school partners at our partnership conference in the summer term prior to the course starting. This way, the course provides information on the up-to-date national educational issues required by trainees and, in partnership with colleagues, the regionally specific interests and challenges that face our partner schools.

Where we differ from our international counterparts, as with many providers and routes in England, is in the length of time it takes to qualify as a teacher. Qualification routes in Norway and South Korea run for five and four years, respectively. There are many advantages to this, not only more time available to study your academic subject, but also time to reflect and critique literature. To ensure that we provide ample opportunity for trainees to become effective consumers of research, we place significant emphasis on engaging with research and, as such, produce high-calibre trainees who can critically engage with school staff, their peers and educational research. Sir Andrew Carter in his review of ITT in 2015 wrote that 'it is critical that ITT should teach trainees why engaging with research is important and build an expectation and enthusiasm for teaching as an evidence-based profession' (Carter, 2015: 22). We champion research in action with a yearly conference, our own journal and our own blog, which encourages staff and trainees to contribute to research and reflect upon their practice. Our MA in Professional Education then takes this one step further and provides the opportunity to convert the 90 CAT points gained during the PGCE into a full MA in Professional Education. Teaching has been explicitly promoted as a research- and evidence-informed profession on both a bottom-up and top-down basis since 1996 (Cordingley, 2015), and at Warwick we create a course which emphasises this.

In order to ensure subject excellence, we dedicate course time to subject knowledge and provide subject specific experts for all of our PGCE Core courses. In a review of research behind effective teaching, Coe et al. (2014) found that a teacher's subject knowledge and their understanding of how pupils handle this subject has the strongest evidence of impact on student outcomes. And so we focus on ensuring subject expertise, and have a proven track record of engaging our university colleagues from departments such as modern foreign languages, chemistry and life sciences in the subject-knowledge component of the course. Partnership of all types is at the forefront of everything we do and school colleagues regularly contribute to our yearly programme, as experts in their subject, and their contribution is recognised and rewarded. 'Involving schools and the profession more broadly in the important work of training and inducting teachers into the professions is one of the biggest positive difference to teaching practice over the last decade' (Crisp, 2017: 11).

Days at university are split between subject studies and reflective practice and throughout the year we move through the teacher standards, using the expert knowledge of our staff to emphasise national issues such as PREVENT, mental wellbeing of young people, safeguarding and progress, as well as literacy and numeracy, behaviour management, technology-enhanced learning, assessment, feedback and differentiation.

We create an excellent and effective course for our trainees, who rate us as well over the sector averages for teaching, engagement, assessment and many other course aspects reported on by the Postgraduate Taught Experience Survey (Figure 7.1).

As well as excellence in terms of course-quality grade, we also effectively support our trainees in their search for employment, with 84 per cent of 2016/17 trainees gaining work within our partner schools, postcodes B, CV or LE, re-emphasising the positive partnership we have with over 595 schools across all routes (Figure 7.2). We

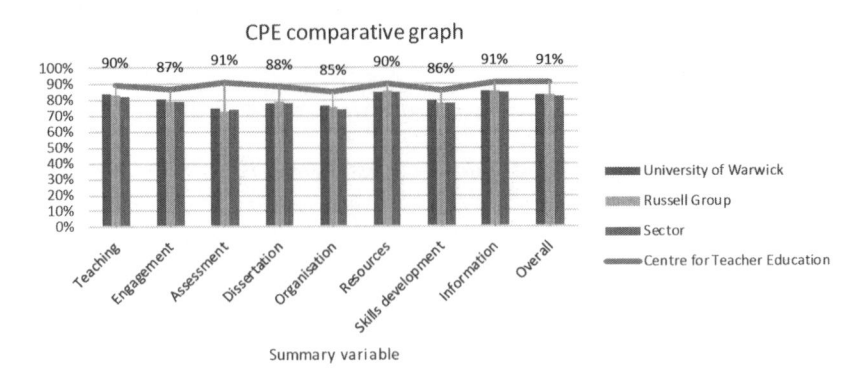

FIGURE 7.1 Comparison of PTES results

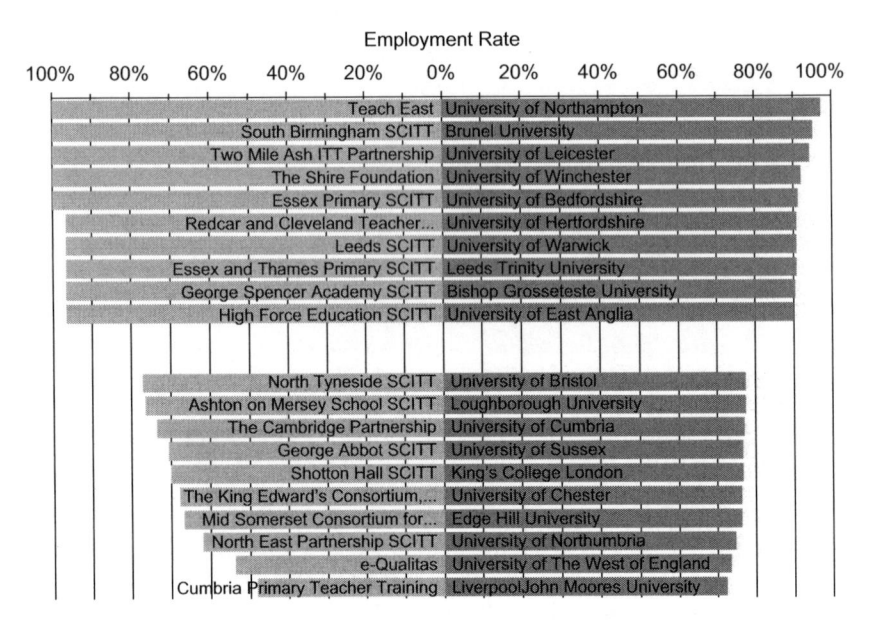

FIGURE 7.2 Providers with the highest and lowest employment rates
Source: DfE, 2018c

are also in the top 10 higher education institute providers for employment rates, according to the 2018 Department for Education report.

And, of course, we provide excellent outcomes for trainees, with 95 per cent of trainees in 2017/18 achieving good or outstanding teacher status, receiving positive trainee evaluations for both university- and school-led aspects of the course (Figure 7.3).

In comparison again to our international counterparts, the advantage for teachers training in this country may be the prolonged 120 minimum teaching days in schools. Courses in Norway and South Korea, as previously discussed, only provide new teachers with 110 days of school experience in total. This sustained time in schools provides the hands-on experience so vital for developing classroom presence and confidence. It is possible to suggest that intensive PGCE courses can lead to trainee burn out, with the shock factor of such a high classroom demand so early on leading to significant drop-out rates (Figure 7.4).

However, at Warwick we have excellent trainee retention rates due to the focussed support from tutors, school-based mentors and student support services. There are overarching government plans to address issues of retention (DfE, 2018c) and we are committed to continuing professional development as one of the many

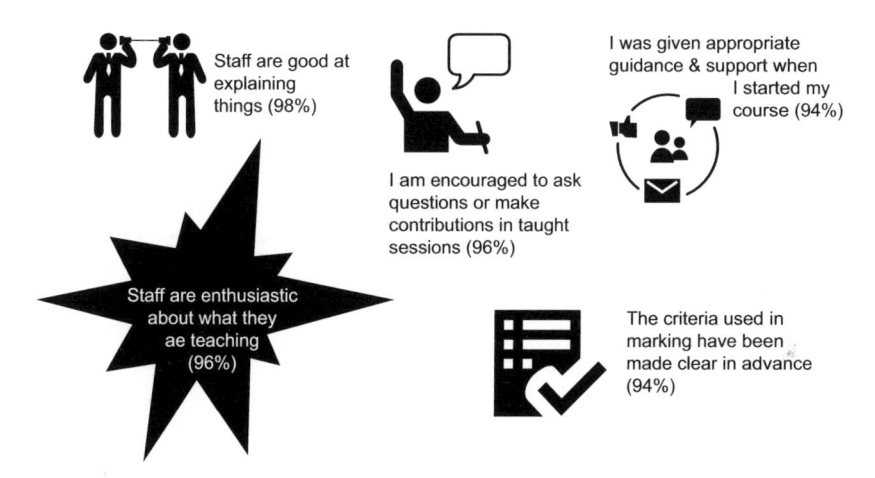

Staff are good at explaining things (98%)

I am encouraged to ask questions or make contributions in taught sessions (96%)

I was given appropriate guidance & support when I started my course (94%)

Staff are enthusiastic about what they ae teaching (96%)

The criteria used in marking have been made clear in advance (94%)

FIGURE 7.3 2017 Postgraduate Taught Experience Survey results

The workload on my course has been manageable (66%)

FIGURE 7.4 2017 Postgraduate Taught Experience Survey results

possible solutions. Significant numbers of our trainees continue to complete our MA or other professional development courses at Warwick, as well as our own in-house mentor training to support new trainees swapping roles. Teachers typically develop faster in the first years in the classroom than when more experienced (Kraft and Papay, 2014) and alongside our well-trained professional team of mentors in schools, we provide a supportive NQT programme of events to support classroom practice. We also have a member of staff teaching on our course with expertise in educational professional development.

Many of our school colleagues and NQTs engage in these collaborative research-based learning opportunities, both with our staff and our current trainees and present at our partnership conference in June, or our Research in Action conference in December. It is accepted that some activities can help you develop faster than others (Cordingley et al., 2015), including those that are collaborative and research-led. Many trainees, school and university staff choose to write articles for our *Warwick Journal of Education – Transforming Teaching* and our blog: 'engaging in this form of activity allows trainees to begin to view themselves as engaged in the teaching profession and with activities that are valued in the research community' (Mawson, 2017).

The creation of the Early Career Framework and the reduced timetable for NQTs in their second year of induction, both outcomes of the Department for Education consultation on extending QTS, will help to ensure that the trainees we send into schools as NQTs can effectively engage with the process of early career development and become the informed, engaged recently qualified teachers schools and their students deserve. We look forward to engaging with these developments, as well as continuing to support trainees in their journey into teaching in a university-led, school-focussed setting.

Case study 2: secondary trainee

A student perspective of the PGCE SD Secondary English programme is provided by Laura Meyrick.

As part of my teacher training programme, I predominantly trained in one school, with a short-term complementary placement at another school within the area. We attended university every Friday and had a teaching timetable at our main school Monday to Thursday. Before we started our training programme, we had a week in August before the term started, where we were at university on an induction programme to teacher training. During this week we were introduced to the eight teaching standards which were broken down, alongside examples of how we can successfully evidence each standard. We also had the opportunity to meet our subject lead and other trainee teachers who were training to teach our subject. As I was an English trainee, our subject group was quite large. This was beneficial as we all had degrees in a variety of English expertise, which allowed us to share our knowledge. This week also helped us by giving us an insight into what to expect from the course, such as our assignments, online evidence portfolio and credits towards our master's qualification.

Our training programme was designed so that schools were able to train and shape young trainee teachers. For the first two weeks, I had a timetable at my school to follow which meant that I had the opportunity to settle in, have some introductory meetings and essential training sessions in order for me to work in the school and to understand school policies and procedures. After the initial fortnight, I had a timetable in English which consisted of several lesson observations of various members of the department. These observations were incredibly useful as I was able to pick up techniques to manage behaviour for learning, as well as key teaching and learning techniques. I was able to observe groups from Key Stage 3 up to Key Stage 5. For some of these observations, I was given certain things to look out for and had to discuss my findings with my mentor, and we were able to discuss how I could implement these teaching and learning strategies within the schemes of work.

After the first month of settling in, I was given nine hours of teaching. I had seven hours of Year 7 teaching and two hours of Year 9 teaching. This was a big leap from only observing to then teaching nine hours a week. I met regularly with my mentor each week, where we would create detailed lesson plans and then she would set me some tasks to do with my planning, to ensure that I had thoroughly planned my lessons. During the spring term, my teaching time increased to 12 hours as I inherited three hours of Year 10 lessons. This allowed me to gain experience with Key Stage 4 teaching with support from my mentor. As I became more confident with my teaching, my timetable increased to 15 hours, with some observing of Year 13, time in the Student Support Centre and taking on a Year 8 group once a week. This gradual increase in my timetable meant that I wasn't overwhelmed with teaching, and the way the Key Stages were introduced meant that I was given time to build my confidence in the previous Key Stage. However, I would have really liked to have been introduced to Year 10/11 teaching at an earlier stage in my training year so that I could have had more experience before my NQT year.

During the year, our subject sessions on a Friday at university supported our timetable changes, as we were each given certain schemes of work to plan, alongside doing a subject knowledge audit on a weekly basis and incorporating cross-curricular skills. Conducting sessions on cross-curricular learning was incredibly useful as it allowed me to work with trainees in other subjects to teach a topic through incorporating a variety of subjects. We created a lesson on World War One which incorporated English, music, history, drama and science. I took this experience to my own teaching as I included some drama whilst teaching poetry, included some historical facts before reading a text and some geographical context about a time period we were studying. Having this experience whilst at university allowed us all to experiment with incorporating a variety of subjects and tasks into a lesson. Also, we had the opportunity to adopt the role of students experiencing the lessons, which was a great opportunity.

Moreover, we had to have a placement at a complementary school to allow us to have experience in a different type of school. My placement was quite short here, but I gained experience teaching A-level from a different specification, which meant that I could develop my teaching and learning knowledge. I also conducted some Year 11 language intervention sessions, which meant that I had the opportunity to trial different teaching techniques for intervention sessions. Additionally, the texts I was teaching and the GCSE specifications were different to my main placement school, which increased my subject knowledge further.

Similarly, we had to experience teaching in a primary school. During my placement at primary I was able to work with Key Stage 1 and Key Stage 2 staff and students. I was able to observe the teaching at different Key Stages as well as have an in-depth look at the marking across both Key Stages. Whilst there, I had the opportunity to work with small groups of students in a variety of different subjects, which was very valuable as I was able to see the journey from Key Stage 1 up to Key Stage 5. This particular part of the course inspired my job role currently, as I am heavily involved with the transition from Key Stage 2 to Key Stage 3. Despite this, I feel that having more time in a primary school would have been more constructive, in order to fully witness the style of teaching and learning which could then be compared to secondary teaching.

A vital element of the training course was the prospect of a research study to go towards a Master's in Educational Innovation. To gain credits towards the master's accreditation, we had to conduct a two-part research study on a topic of our choice. I based my research study on literacy and grammar as this was, and still is, a passion of mine. I looked at the teaching of grammar in isolation and the impact it had on improving students' literacy skills. Completing the master's as part of my teacher training course meant that I could acquire experience as an academic writer through completing in-depth research and applying it into my teaching practice. It also inspired me to continue with my master's research alongside my teaching in my NQT year, to achieve a full master's accreditation which subsequently was published by the University of Warwick in the *Transforming Teaching* journal.

Overall, my teacher training course consisted of a variety of elements to ensure that I had experienced a variety of teaching styles, working in different schools, and the opportunity to develop my subject knowledge through academic research.

Conclusion

The contributions by university staff and trainee teachers to this chapter illustrate the range of programmes available and the changing nature of the relationship between schools and HE institutions. There appears to be some blurring of the different routes, and it is clear that the relationship between schools and HE continues to evolve, with greater responsibility being given to schools. HE staff have had to be pragmatic to retain any involvement in the training of teachers. However, HE does continue to play a role and it is attempting to articulate a clear purpose.

As we argued earlier, teacher education has always been located heavily in school in addition to HE. As the boundaries change, HE staff have increasingly been forced to justify their role. One area which HE staff have identified as being under their control is developing the link between research and practice in developing new teachers (Maguire, 2014). To support this, HE teacher training programmes operate at master's level, and trainee teachers are encouraged to continue to study for a master's-level qualification as part of their ongoing professional development (Brant and Vincent, 2017). Exposure to a range of different teaching approaches based on research, and the development of a profession that takes research evidence seriously, would appear to be key roles for university-based teacher educators.

8

MODELS OF PROVISION

School-based

Introduction

In previous chapters, we have documented and described the continuing expectation placed on schools to play a greater role in the training of teachers. This is part of the continuing process designed to fragment the education system, especially as new providers have been encouraged to enter the education market, with new ways to manage and operate schools (Middlewood and Abbott, 2017). According to Blatchford and Gash (2012: 5), this will ensure that 'innovative organisations will step forward to provide public services in new ways, and competition will force performing providers to up their game or face failure'.

In this chapter, we consider models of school-based provision from the perspective of the schools involved. Schools tend to be involved in a number of different training schemes, working with a range of partners. Our examples will consider all aspects of the process, from recruitment to ongoing staff development for newly qualified teachers (NQTs) following qualification. In particular, we look at the practical implications of school-based teacher training and how it impacts on staff and school students. School staff have been required to take on a number of roles and responsibilities that, in the past, have been undertaken by higher education (HE)-based tutors. The accounts have been written by staff in schools and are written from their perspective, based on their day-to-day experiences of working with trainee teachers. Both schools have had issues recruiting sufficient high-quality teachers. The first account provides an insight into the realities and myriad of routes of school-based teacher training in a recently established large inner-city secondary academy school.

Secondary

Background

I originally trained as a modern foreign languages teacher, before becoming head of department and then taking on several responsibilities within the remit of teaching and learning. I trained to be a teacher through the PGCE route, subsequently completing a master's in teaching at the Institute of Education. At school, I currently lead on continuing professional development and initial teacher training (ITT) and work as an associate tutor on the master's of teaching course in my spare time.

I work in an inner-city London academy. The academy itself is part of a national academy chain but operates largely on an independent basis, having total control of its own policies and curriculum. The school has approximately 1,100 students, of which the majority are classified as pupil premium. There are over 40 different languages spoken and although the catchment area of the school is small, it is very diverse, with a wide range of ethnicities.

The school has a strong focus on teaching and learning, and is very proud of the quality of the in-house training and ability to develop teachers. We are a start-up academy and therefore have had a strong focus on recruitment over the last five years. This has led to us recruiting experienced teachers and unqualified and NQTs through a variety of training programmes. We currently have teachers training through Teach First, school-based teacher training (run by an outstanding academy chain) and NQTs.

From a school perspective, trainees are categorised into two groups:

- NQTs;
- unqualified teachers, i.e. teachers who have had no previous teacher training.

All teachers, regardless of level, take part in a comprehensive induction programme which starts in the summer term, with one day of training focussed on the school's teaching and learning handbook and approach to the curriculum. NQTs are then invited to work for two weeks during the summer term to observe lessons and school routines and where possible take part in co-teaching. Unqualified teachers are also encouraged to come in and observe as much as possible; indeed, this is a requirement on the training schemes we run and is classified as school orientation. At the end of August, all new teachers attend an induction programme of between two and four days.

This training includes introductions to the key school policies and how to implement them, e.g. behaviour systems, lesson planning and classroom techniques. This is followed up with weekly after-school training sessions for all new teachers (these sessions are in addition to anything offered by the different training routes and are a requirement for all new teachers at the school). Finally, every new teacher receives a 'leverage mentor' for at least the first term. Trainee teachers have this entitlement for the whole year. This is a mentor who observes the trainee teacher every week for 15 minutes and gives feedback in the form of the highest leverage action point which must then be implemented in the following week.

Our trainee teachers also attend a weekly 30-minute meeting dedicated to their specific development. NQTs and unqualified teachers attend different meetings, each run by a senior, experienced teacher. These meetings cover a wide variety of topics, to help induct and develop trainees into school life. For example, one session may cover whole staff training in more detail, or focus on day-to-day responsibilities such as doing your first parents' evening, making phone calls home or the role of form tutors.

Training routes

Post-Graduate Certificate of Education

The secondary PGCE takes a year to complete at an HE institution and comprises two teaching placements in different secondary schools. Students complete a number of assignments over the year which are of master's level, and credits can be carried forward and put towards a master's qualification at a later date. This was the route I followed when I took the decision to leave the corporate sector to become a teacher.

Teach First

The school has a number of Teach First alumni and whilst we recognise this as a very effective training route, we try to recruit independently before using the Teach First route, believing that Teach First trainees should be placed in schools where the need is greatest. Teach First provides a comprehensive training and support package for trainees that operates alongside the normal school routines. They require trainees to have a certain number of days out of school for training, which has minimal cover implications (approximately one day per half term plus a week at a contrasting school). Trainees are observed by Teach First tutors and subject-specific tutors in addition to their school mentor. Teach First trainees are employed initially on a two-year contract, i.e. it is intended that they complete their ITT year and NQT year at the same school. Teach First participants qualify with a Post-Graduate Diploma in Education and Leadership and complete master's-level assignments.

School-based initial teacher training

This training route requires considerably more involvement from the school to support teacher training than the two routes mentioned above. Trainees are required to spend half a day every week with the training provider and have a range of placements that need to be completed at other schools (approximately 20 days over the course of the year). This is supplemented with two observations per half term and a requirement for weekly timetabled co-teaching and co-planning support. Trainees on this route may choose whether to opt in to the PGCE qualification, although they are encouraged to. Our ITT route includes trainees on the Now Teach programme who train on a part-time (80 per cent) basis.

Newly qualified teachers

We typically recruit between six and ten NQTs every year. A proportion of these may be teachers who have completed their ITT at the school, but for training purposes all NQTs are treated the same. We have recruited from a range of universities and take into account the standard and Ofsted rating of the university's PGCE course and subject specialism. NQTs at our school qualify through the National Induction Panel for Teachers, which we have found to be very cost-efficient and to have effective organisation.

Strengths and weaknesses

In my experience, the PGCE route produces the most varied cohort of NQTs. Assignments completed during the course are of master's standard and, therefore, graduates tend to have a deeper pedagogical understanding of education and how to teach in theory, but less practice than those following the other routes into teaching. PGCE courses also do not tend to stipulate a one-size-fits-all approach to lesson planning and curriculum writing, which affords for more creativity and independence in their approach to teaching. This also means that NQTs may lack some skills in the practicality of writing schemes of work and in considering how a series of lessons fit together. The development and strengths and weaknesses of a PGCE student are very much dependent on the quality of their mentors in their training schools and the type of school they are placed in. In practice, this means that graduates have a very varied and inconsistent skill base when they start their NQT year. To date, we have not had any PGCE placements at the academy, therefore all recruits through this process have completed placements at alternate secondary schools.

Our recruitment process focusses on assessing the self-reflective nature of teachers and their openness to feedback and induction programmes fills gaps they may have in the more day-to-day issues, such as behaviour management. As we are confident in these processes, an NQT's creativity, independence and varied teaching background can be a real asset to a department and lead to original teaching ideas and engaging lessons. However, where they have not completed a placement in a fast-paced inner-city academy, there is a very steep learning curve (hence the need for self-reflectiveness and openness!). NQTs must adapt quickly and be responsive to feedback, implementing action points straight away. The weekly 30-minute NQT meeting has been invaluable in helping this group to adapt. It gives NQTs a safe place to discuss and share ideas and get the additional support they need to be successful.

In considering the unqualified routes, there is no doubt that the general calibre of those recruited through the Teach First scheme is higher than the other routes.

This may be due to the high profile of the Teach First brand, or their targeting of students from Russell Group universities. This is particularly shown through the proactive nature of Teach First participants and their ability to hit the ground running and teach independently from day one. I have also noticed a positive change in the attitudes of Teach First trainees over the past few years. Whilst trainees on this route are generally motivated by their desire to help students from disadvantaged backgrounds and create positive social change, they have also become more focussed on working as part of the existing team in a school and follow a more collaborative approach in recent years.

We are fortunate that the school-based training provider we use also focusses on a trainee's ability to be self-reflective during their recruitment process. This quality is one of the most important to have as a teacher, as the ability to accurately reflect on your lesson (both what went well and areas of improvement) is vital to a successful training year. However, what is really important is not only the importance of reflection, but then being able to act on these reflections. This ability to act is sometimes omitted through other school-based training routes. What often holds trainees back is their inability to act upon these reflections and in some cases being too overly negative with their reflections. The purpose of our leverage mentoring programme is to give trainees easily actionable development points which will have a direct impact on the classroom. An example of these might be to script an introduction to a task, a positive behaviour-management technique or clear lesson timings. The ability for a trainee to act on these directly correlates to their effectiveness in the classroom and therefore needs to be accurately assessed during the recruitment of trainee teachers. Whilst this takes a considerable time commitment from experienced teaching staff in school, we have found it to be the most successful way to develop trainees. We also have technology available whereby you can video your lesson and watch it back, to help with this reflection process.

Both the Teach First and school-based ITT routes follow a very formulaic route approach to teacher training and teach specific formats for lesson planning and behaviour management. They follow a tried and tested formula that enables trainees to manage difficult behaviour effectively and deliver and plan lessons using a standard format (as agreed by the training provider). This approach allows trainees to plan and teach straight away (as opposed to the PGCE which often sees students just observing for the first few weeks of their placement). This approach is certainly effective in behaviour management and produces teachers who are able to competently deal with the behaviour demands of an inner-city school. However, trainees following these routes do not appear to have the same breadth of pedagogical understanding of how learning works, or as broad a range of lesson-planning ideas and approaches as those who have followed the PGCE route. Whilst the approach they follow is effective, deviating from this approach can be problematic for some trainees. A good example of this is when we recruited for a new modern foreign languages teacher a couple of years ago and interviewed three previous Teach First participants, who had graduated in three different cohorts but planned and taught the exact same lesson at interview. Unless teachers are able to move beyond this formulaic approach, their development opportunities are limited. However, it must be acknowledged that these training routes are getting teachers into schools that really need them and that in itself can only be a positive thing, given the challenges many schools experience in recruiting suitable staff.

Regardless of the training route, all trainees require more support and time from experienced teachers than recruiting qualified teachers. However, the process of training teachers is certainly a worthwhile development opportunity for existing members of staff. Mentoring and coaching a trainee helps you to reflect and improve on your own practice and keeps the conversation of teaching and learning at the top of the agenda. Mentors need to be given directed time through the timetable in order to support trainees and NQTs, and some thought needs to be given to the pairing of mentors with trainees to allow them to reach their potential. Where a trainee has been less successful, it can usually (at least partly) be attributed to a breakdown on the mentor–mentee relationship and/or lack of time to adequately support their development. On this basis, mentor and co-planning meetings need to be protected time in the timetable where possible and prioritised.

Our school policy is that all teachers will have at least one observation every term and there is a non-hierarchical approach to lesson observations, which means a trainee is just as likely to be observed by a vice principal as to be observing one. This focus on lesson observation creates a shared knowledge of what makes an excellent lesson and allows all best practice to be shared easily throughout the school. This culture of openness around lesson observations undoubtedly helps our trainees to develop and progress quicker than if they were just isolated in their own classrooms. It also ensures there is no stigma attached to lessons observations and they are quickly normalised, as just part of teachers' continuing professional development entitlement.

There are also other school approaches that help us to effectively train new teachers, particularly the focus co-planning. It is standard that departments will have at least one weekly co-planning meeting, entirely focussed on planning and delivering lessons as opposed to a general department meeting. This allows teachers to discuss the learning value of lesson activities and to discuss how to actually teach them. This collaborative approach enables trainees to get feedback on any lessons they have planned in advance and, where they are teaching a lesson planned by another teacher, ensure they have a thorough understanding of how to teach the lesson, including some scripting. This process is not 100 per cent dictatorial and teachers are able to adapt/change lessons to suit their preferences as required.

Other factors to consider

As in any school, there are more difficulties in recruiting in certain subjects such as science and maths. However, we have learnt from experience that teachers following the school-based teacher training route are not substitutes for qualified teachers and, to succeed, need to have an option to be able to teach with support in all lessons from the outset, rather than assuming their ability to teach independently from day one. Therefore, I would suggest that unqualified teachers are recruited in addition to the school's required teaching staff requirement.

For trainees on the school-based ITT route, they are required to apply for a full-time job during their training year. Where a candidate decides not to apply, or is unsuccessful in the recruitment process, this can lead to challenges around trainee motivation and engagement for the remainder of the year and this process must be handled sensitively and transparently.

We have been fortunate to have a number of high-quality teaching assistants and learning support assistants (TAs/LSAs), who have gone on to train via various teacher training routes at our school. There is no doubt that this puts the trainee at a massive advantage and certainly the majority of our most successful trainees have come through this route. High aspirations are part of our school culture and we are also keen to encourage potential teachers by including our TAs/LSAs in the ITT induction programme and giving them opportunities to observe and co-teach in lessons during their time as a TA/LSA, to nurture talent. This is an excellent way to recruit future trainees as we already know that they are in line with the school's culture and mission statement.

The second case study illustrates some of the issues arising in the primary sector from the development of school-based teacher training. In this case the school was already well established in a market town but converted to become an academy as part of a larger chain in 2013.

Primary

School Direct: Nene and Ramnoth School, Wisbech

Nene and Ramnoth School is a good school in the heart of Wisbech. We are very proud of our school. Our team of teachers, teaching assistants and governors are committed to ensuring that our children will achieve success, enjoy their education and become confident, active learners. On 1 October 2013, we converted to be part of the Elliot Foundation Academy Trust. At this time we were Nene Infant and Nursery School and Ramnoth Junior School, but at that point we federated and so Nene and Ramnoth School was born! We currently offer one school on two sites – an early years base and a Key Stage 1 and Key Stage 2 base. We are expanding to become three-form entry in each year group and this has led to a fantastic new building programme on our Key Stage 1 and Key Stage 2 site. This expansion and building project has been funded by our local authority and means we are able to offer a high-quality learning environment for our children.

We have been working with the School of Education at the University of Bedfordshire and one of their School Direct partners (Fenland Teaching School Alliance) to provide placements for trainee teachers for the last two years. During this time, we have developed strong links with the School of Education and share their educational ethos. We are delighted that the School of Education has accepted us to become a School Direct partner from September 2018. The University of

Bedfordshire is one of the largest education providers in the UK. The university has a long, established and proven record of training teachers and in many cases they have a 100 per cent graduate employment rate. If a trainee successfully completes the course, they will be recommended for qualified teacher status (QTS) to the National College for Teaching and Leadership.

Nene and Ramnoth School is the lead school for School Direct with the eastern region of the Elliot Foundation Academy Trust. We follow the principles of the Elliot Foundation and provide education for children between the ages of 2–11 years old. We are supported by partnership schools from the Elliot Foundation (eastern region) and the Wisbech Schools Partnership, where the trainee's teaching experience will take place. The schools within our partnership for this academic year are:

- Alderman Payne Primary School, Parson Drove
- Elm Road Primary School, Wisbech
- Eyrescroft Primary School, Peterborough
- Friday Bridge Primary School, Wisbech
- Highlees Primary School, Peterborough
- Millfield Primary School, Littleport
- Peckover Primary School, Wisbech
- Ramnoth Junior School, Wisbech.

Together, we are committed to providing high-quality training, where our trainees spend time in schools learning from our dedicated and committed teachers. We will provide excellent guidance and support in order to find the right school for each trainee, to give good classroom environments to practise and refine their professional skills. Trainees will have the opportunity to undertake placements that will provide a variety of experiences, both academic and pastoral. We will tailor our provision to meet the needs of our trainee teachers to enable them to have the best possible start to their teaching career.

When selecting trainees for the School Direct PGCE Primary we are looking for those who have:

- commitment to teaching and a desire to be an outstanding teacher;
- excellent communication, organisational skills and flexibility in an active and constantly changing environment;
- enthusiasm and commitment to working hard, as part of a professional team;
- the ability to establish good working relationships with children and staff;
- confidence and ability to engage with children;
- a desire to work in the eastern region.

School Direct, through the University of Bedfordshire, offers graduates the chance to gain QTS whilst on school placements throughout the year. Trainees are placed in schools within the partnership area and we aim to provide them with a range of opportunities in different high-quality placement settings that are well matched to a trainee's developmental needs. The university ensures that all Primary trainees have taught in at least two schools, with placements in at least one Key Stage 1 setting and one Key Stage 2 setting, for a specified number of days. Primary trainees are required to teach all core and foundation subjects. Trainees will need to be assessed as meeting all of the standards for QTS across the specified age range of their training. Trainees will not be awarded QTS until they have met all of the QTS standards. University staff visit the trainees whilst they are on school placements, as the university is accountable for all assessment judgements and recommendations for QTS.

From September 2018, we will be providing our own placements for School Direct training; to date two trainees have been recruited for placements with us. As part of the recruitment process, the School Direct lead invites the trainees into school to tour, share the ethos and vision of the school, meet the staff team and, alongside the executive principal, the trainee is observed working with a class of children – teaching an activity related to a book of the trainee's choice. The School Direct lead also attends the PGCE Primary interviews at the University of Bedfordshire as part of the university recruitment and interview process.

As part of the School Direct process, all trainees on placement are provided with a high-quality mentor, who is responsible for making judgements/assessments about a trainee's competency against the Teachers' Standards. As trainees are expected to complete a specified number of days on placement, it is important that strong links are maintained with the university and concerns about attendance and suitability for teaching must be raised at an early stage. Trainees are assessed through weekly observations in order to maintain consistency in meeting the Teachers' Standards. The mentor is expected to complete all relevant documents and detail both targets for trainees and the support provided to help them to develop their practice. In some placements the class teacher and the mentor are the same person, but it is possible that the mentor will not always be the class teacher.

We have successfully used a very experienced vice principal as our School Direct mentor for trainee placements within our school for the last two years and this has ensured high-quality provision for our trainees. Our mentor works closely with the class teacher to ensure that they gain a complete view of the trainee's progress. As part of this process, the trainee's planning for teaching is monitored and assessed, weekly meetings are held with the trainee when progress is discussed and support offered for their wider professional development and the mentor completes the mentor records and the profile review point, which reports on the trainee's progress towards the achievement of defined standards of teaching. Whilst this can become a time-consuming process, experience has shown that this quality time with the mentor has enabled our trainees to be successful in gaining QTS.

As the class teacher is not the trainee's mentor, it has allowed a different sort of working relationship between the trainee and the class teacher. The class teacher is able to support the trainee to focus on the day-to-day planning and preparation for individuals, group and whole-class teaching, and offer guidance, support and assistance with assessment. The class teacher acts as a role model, with the trainee working alongside them, following the planning and framework provided by the teacher. Informal feedback is regularly provided by the class teacher. Support is provided on the use of the class data system, assessment and record-keeping systems, to ensure that our trainees have a good understanding of our requirements. As the trainee becomes more confident they begin to plan their own lessons, with support from the class teacher. As the placement progresses, the trainees can be given greater freedom to devise appropriate learning objectives and activities for the lessons that they are going to deliver.

Our class teacher offers both supported teaching and guided teaching to our trainees. Through supported teaching, the trainee begins to plan their own lessons, this alongside the teacher to ensure that both have input into the identified objectives, methods, activities, etc. The trainee is then able to teach most (or all) of the lesson, with the class teacher observing and assisting. Guided teaching enables the trainee to put forward a plan for the lesson and then modify it with the class teacher's advice before the lesson is delivered. This gives the opportunity for the trainee to take the main responsibility for the teaching of the lesson, with the class teacher adopting the role of teaching assistant by working with identified children, agreed prior to the lesson. As the placement progresses, the trainee can devise appropriate learning objectives and activities for the lessons for which they are responsible, as preparation for their future independent teaching. When our class teacher and mentor feel that the trainee is able to commence independent teaching, the trainee then takes responsibility for the planning and teaching of their lessons. The level of supervision that is needed will be based upon the competency and experience of the trainee. With both our School Direct trainees we have been able to allow them to move on to independent teaching fairly promptly, as working alongside the class teacher in a teaching role has been very successful.

Our trainees have participated in open assemblies for parents, parent consultations and school fundraising events. Whilst on placement with us our trainees are encouraged to embrace school life fully, in order to become a full and effective member of the staff team. They work closely with their class teacher and have opportunities for team teaching, supporting identified groups or individuals, utilising their strengths, whilst at the same time helping them to develop areas where they feel less confident.

Trainees spend four days per week in their placement schools and one day a week at the university. Initially, our trainees spend time observing current teachers during their classes. This enables them to become familiar with the school and the teaching practices that are already used. Over the year, as a trainee's skills and confidence develop, the amount of teaching time will increase. Once the trainees become familiar with the class, we agree a specific area of teaching as a focus for observations.

Teaching at the university is through lectures, seminars and workshops, with opportunities for working independently and collaboratively. There are course assignments, but no formal examinations and the continuous assessment of teaching is based on achieving the national standards for QTS, specified in the most recent government documentation.

We are committed to providing a friendly and accessible service for our trainees. Trainees who have a disability should inform us when making their application so that they can be supported through the recruitment process and be considered for placements at appropriate schools if they are successful at interview.

School Direct has enabled us to train, support and recruit teachers that have a passion for working with our children. This route into teaching allows trainees to gain experience in two different settings and to learn and craft their teaching skills in a very supportive environment. We are delighted that for two years running the School Direct trainees on placement with us have been appointed as NQTs to our school.

One obvious downside of the School Direct route into teaching is that generally it is a non-salaried route. Therefore, this has cost implications for the trainees, as they are expected to work for a year unpaid. For some trainees this route is cost-prohibitive – with the university fees, loans to pay these fees and no income for a year, many trainees cannot consider this route into teaching. Currently there is one salaried School Direct place through a different school lead and this place was filled very quickly. Many enquiries are received about salaried places and unfortunately these prospective trainees have to be advised to try elsewhere, which limits the number of trainees available for school leads to take on our School Direct (Primary) route.

In our area of Fenland, we now have two School Direct lead schools trying to recruit the same trainees. In previous years there may have been six trainees split between one or two providers; for September 2018, the available candidates were able to choose between the three providers within our region. The University of Bedfordshire was recently approached and asked to consider taking on another Wisbech school as a School Direct partner. Fortunately, the university shared our concerns about having another School Direct partner in Wisbech. It is difficult to tell at present whether this will support increasing recruitment in the Wisbech area, or whether the number of recruits will simply be split between the two partners. The university education team are working hard to support us, but they are finding recruitment in the Wisbech area challenging. It would therefore not be in the best interests of the Wisbech schools to further increase the number of School Direct partners until the university can ensure that the current School Direct partners are viable, and they can therefore provide ITT in Wisbech.

When we take our first trainees in September 2018, we aim to provide our future School Direct trainee teachers with excellent guidance and support, in order to give them the best possible start to their teaching career. Schools within the Nene and Ramnoth School/Elliot Foundation eastern region, will be keen to recruit graduates on successful completion of their School Direct PGCE. It is our desire to train teachers in our own local schools and keep them teaching within the local area. Recruitment to Fenland is not easy and by looking after our trainees and supporting them to be the best teachers they can be, we hope that we will benefit from the time we have spent nurturing them, when they are successfully interviewed and recruited to our local schools. Our intention is to develop and retain 'outstanding' teachers of the future.

Conclusion

In both cases, there is a strong desire to produce high-quality teachers and an awareness of the importance of the school in the training process. There is also a recognition that local needs are important from a school's perspective, especially in being able to recruit and retain sufficient teachers for their own needs. This has to be balanced against wider planning considerations, related to ensuring sufficient numbers are trained who adequately represent a diverse population (Maguire and George, 2017). There seems to be little desire from the schools to train restricted professionals and they are keen to ensure that trainee teachers have a wide range of experience, with professional development as a priority. Clearly, the schools want to produce 'outstanding' teachers, but a key question is, what constitutes an outstanding teacher?

These two limited examples provide a recognition of a continuing but developing role for HE within initial teacher education. There is clear value in a wide variety of experiences being offered to trainee teachers, whatever the location of their training programme, despite fears of a narrowing of experience. Appropriate support from a range of professionals is also important and, similarly to HE-based programmes, the role of the school mentor is of crucial importance in securing a successful outcome for trainee teachers, whatever the training route. Effective and secure support from a wide range of school and HE staff is also seen as a key component of a successful training programme. As we noted earlier, the roles of school and HE staff will continue to evolve as school-based programmes develop.

9
TEACH FIRST

We described earlier the rise of alternative routes into teacher education outside the traditional higher education (HE)-led programmes. Perhaps the highest profile of the alternative providers has been Teach First which recruited its first cohort in 2003. Teach First aims to recruit from the 'top universities' and to establish 'high levels of exclusivity' (Wigdortz, 2012: 124 and 127), with an emphasis on developing leadership. This has led to criticism of the scheme because of a movement away from 'specialist knowledge and skills, and towards a more generalised understanding of teaching as a graduate entry profession' (Southern, 2018: 3). However, it is hard to disagree with the mission of Teach First to reduce educational disadvantage and to raise the status of teaching.

In what follows, Reuben Moore and Jennifer Barker from Teach First describe the origins and the development of the charity.

The history

Teach First is a charity whose vision is that no child's educational success is limited by their socio-economic status. It came into existence in 2002, taking its first cohort of teachers (called participants) in June 2003. It grew out of a perceived crisis in London schools. It is interesting to note that many valuable educational achievements across the world were borne out of crisis. The massive strides in Ontario's education followed a period of intense industrial action amongst teachers there. In Singapore, the mandate that all teaching in schools needed to be in English meant new methods of teaching and large groups of new teachers were required.

The specific concern in London, though, was the lack of good teachers being retained in the capital and the resultant negative effect on pupil achievement. At the time, many great staff were being recruited from Canada and Australia, but this was neither a permanent or sustainable solution for the capital.

Partnership

From the beginning, Teach First worked within the system and yet it was quite different from other players in the system. As with any new approach, there was a great deal of focus from the sector and beyond on this initiative, some sceptical and others welcoming. Given this environment, Teach First owes a great deal to a significant number of educationalists, school leaders, university leaders and corporate leaders across the system. Many put their reputations 'on the line', either in discussions with schools or with government, because they believed that our intervention would be successful, as it has proved. Canterbury Christ Church University provided the initial teacher education (ITE) element from the beginning and they remain a key provider, working with us and contributing to the development of the programme. In line with our expansion beyond London, our partnership has grown. Apart from Canterbury Christ Church University, the current partnership includes Bath Spa University, University College London/Institute of Education, Birmingham City University, University of Manchester, Sheffield Hallam University and University of Northumbria. The partnership has always focussed on a shared vision, recognition of expertise and robust discussion, to continuously improve the programme and the teachers we develop together.

There were several areas that were unique in 2003 but have since become part of the structural framework for numerous ITE programmes or teacher-preparation programmes across university- and schools-led provision. It is important to mention where Teach First sits in this context. It is essentially a hybrid of the schools-led and the university-led sectors, aiming to capitalise on the strength of subject, phase and research expertise from academics alongside the practical nature of school-based training. Given the need for our teachers to teach from the beginning of September, these crucial elements, alongside the expertise of internal staff, work to become more than the sum of their parts. Engagement and collaboration from all key groups have enabled the development of this hybrid in which teachers gain the essential value of both inputs, since it is only through the effective use of both that we are able to develop classroom 'technicians' into excellent teaching professionals.

The model

Candidates who join the Leadership Development Programme (what we call our ITE Programme) commit to at least two years in a school that serves economically disadvantaged communities. Candidates choose an area of England or Wales and outline the reasons for their choice. The model is essentially demand-led as schools submit their needs in terms of subject and phase. Teach First endeavours to match candidates with their preference and, given our scale and relationships with over 1,000 schools, we can gain an insight into what subjects and phases are required across England and Wales. Having a larger pool of high-quality trainees that are relatively flexible means we are more likely to fill the demand where teachers are needed most.

One difference in 2003 was the recruitment process. Many corporate firms were managing to recruit high numbers of graduates with great potential through 'milk round'-style activities on university campuses. These firms were viewed as highly selective and *the* place for high-quality graduates. We wanted to add teaching to this category, to make training and teaching in a school in a low-income community seen as a job with high prestige; a realistic destination for high-potential graduates who might not have otherwise considered teaching. The resultant focus of the programme was that of leadership development, where graduates could make a real difference in the short term but also build great skills to progress in school or other fields. Even today, our literature focusses on alumni who have gone into different sectors including leadership in schools. It also led us to create a summer institute (SI) and to the decision to give teachers a timetable with full or close to full responsibility from the start. Graduates attracted to the competitor and prestigious programmes from corporations wanted to have responsibility from the beginning.

Candidates apply to Teach First, completing an application and robust assessment centre, as well as other standard admission procedures such as curriculum knowledge audits, fitness to teach and spending five days in a school before the programme begins. The programme starts with a five-week SI. Participants spend time developing subject knowledge, learning about pedagogy, about their local area, practising in school and developing as leaders, building their sense of being a cohort and an understanding of Teach First's vision.

Our trainees then go into their placement school. They are an employee of the school and in their first year are paid as unqualified teachers. Whilst working on a timetable of between 70 and 90 per cent of a newly qualified teacher, they are working towards qualified teacher status (2003 to 2009), towards a PGCE (2010 to 2016) or PGDE (2017–present). They are supported by a participant development lead from Teach First, colleagues from the university and mentors in school. The focus and emphasis of these support roles has changed over time. As well as an academic award, our teachers also gain insights into leadership and into their ability to work within a broad movement aiming to end educational inequality. The balance of the curriculum between teaching and learning, leadership and movement changes throughout the programme. At the end of the two years, many choose to remain in schools (around 60 per cent), others go into complementary fields such as policy or social enterprise and the remainder explore careers elsewhere, including a small number who go into the corporate world. Interestingly, there are more of the 2003 cohort teaching today than in the year after they completed their programme. It is encouraging to see many return to teaching and some going into headship with experience of other sectors to support them leading a school.

Impact

Assessing the impact of any single 'intervention' in education is a very challenging prospect, as so many facets are at play upon pupil, school or system achievement. The Teach First route is just one way into teaching, which blends with other routes and with talented and more experienced colleagues in schools. Many reasons are offered to the relative success story of education in London. Some are within the education sphere and others more to do with the flow of people into the capital. Work by CfBT concluded that Teach First was one of three main interventions which contributed to London's educational success. The others were the collaboration of London Challenge and the academisation programme. It is vital for all teaching routes to try to assess their impact, not just in the time of training but the success of that teacher in the medium term. ITE is a very formative experience and for many teachers the most intense form of professional development that they may receive in their entire career. The impact of that formative experience goes way beyond the training year, and we as a system should be trying to capture that to assess the impact of programmes. At Teach First, we have always been focussed on impact, no matter how difficult it is to monitor, because pupils in all communities deserve a great education.

Teach First has now trained over 10,000 teachers in over 1,700 schools across 11 areas in England and Wales and, to assess the impact of this, we use standard measurements such as retention, quality of qualified teacher status, employability and satisfaction. We constantly evolve and develop the programme to further improve these figures.

Teach First has also had many external evaluations by Ofsted (2003, 2007, 2012, 2015) and the Welsh inspectorate (Estyn, 2015). Inspectors have often commented upon the focus on raising achievement for pupils serving low-income schools, the strength of the partnership and the cohort of teachers. This quote from our 2015 report from London sums this up well: 'Everyone is wedded to the fundamental principle of improving the life chances of disadvantaged pupils. This common goal drives all partners and participants to strive for excellence. Nothing but the best will do.'

Independent research carried out by the Institute of Education (Allen and Allnutt, 2017) found that schools working with Teach First improved their GCSE scores. Researchers compared the results of pupils in Teach First partner schools to those in similar schools without them (including those that partnered with us later). At a schoolwide level, they found that a GCSE student in a school with our teachers improved by one grade overall across their eight best GCSEs. Perhaps more significantly, the report also concluded that the presence of Teach First teachers 'raises the teaching standards of those who teach alongside them in the same department'.

By analysing the GCSE results of departments before partnering with Teach First, the study found that some departments were achieving GCSE grade performances that were 9 per cent lower than other departments within the same school. Yet after partnering with Teach First, these same lower-performing departments then went on to outperform their counterparts by 16 per cent within two years.

We are fortunate that we stay in touch with significant numbers of our alumni. However, this is not by accident. Part of the uniqueness of Teach First is the importance of building a movement and this being a lifelong commitment rather than a time-limited teacher training programme. We have 4,285 alumni working in schools; 1,358 are middle leaders and 328 are senior leaders. We also have 35 headteachers. We support ambassadors in several ways to develop further in school. This might be accessing a subject or phase network, it might be a pathways programme to support a move into middle and senior leadership, it may be referral and signposting to educational leadership programmes or it may be careers coaching and application support for their next step.

The programme

Our programme has gone through many changes since 2003, to respond to data, research and feedback from schools, teachers and universities. In this section, we will explore the underpinning tenets of the programme. We will then explain the changes made in 2017, which have been the most fundamental in our history. There are three elements that have not changed with any of these changes. These are, a focus on teaching and learning, leadership and contributing to a movement focussed on educational inequality.

Teaching and learning

Developing effective teachers for the benefit of pupils in low-income communities sits at the heart of everything we do. This starts with the SI which, given our teachers are employed as substantive class teachers from the beginning of September, has been of vital importance. The careful balance between front-loading content during an intensive SI and spreading this out across the year when schools are understandably reluctant to release their teachers has been a challenging one to manage. We found that the SI offered a series of benefits to participants – content delivery at a time when there is a readiness to absorb it, time before the reality of a timetable kicks in and an opportunity to build a strong cohort culture. Relationships forged in intense periods can often last a lifetime and this is true for Teach First cohorts, judging by the number who work, socialise and live together well beyond the two-year programme. This, however, is balanced by our understanding of how to nurture developing teachers, the need to introduce content in a carefully sequenced way, to ensure a significant opportunity to connect theory to practice and, as described above, the opportunity to practise all elements of planning, assessing, managing behaviour and teaching.

During the SI, teachers also spend time in another school. This was mainly to allow our teachers to see different contexts and outstanding practice. It was also an opportunity for our teachers to teach their challenging first lessons without 'fear' of meeting those pupils in September. Our focus on practice and on rehearsal has sharpened considerably over time but it is interesting to note that, even in 2003, we valued its importance.

Beyond the SI there were six days of university input for secondary and nine for primary and early years, as well as support role visits throughout the year, at least once per half term but commensurate with need. Visits were undertaken by professional and subject tutors from the university. This support was provided in the first year only. In 2009, Teach First introduced a leadership development officer into this mix of professionals. The intention was to provide in-person support throughout the two-year experience, but most significantly in the second year when the university input had ended.

During the early years, there was a significant divide between the SI content and that provided on the additional university input. The six (or nine for primary) days were often in response to the needs of teachers, but as time went on, there was recognition that developing teachers needed specific elements in a sequence for them to develop rapidly. While many of our early teachers are outstanding practitioners, six days of university input was limiting and it was only with the new PGDE that we could think more deeply about the importance of sequencing a programme across two years.

Leadership

Many people associate Teach First with leadership. It is certainly important to the charity and is a foundation in all our programmes (Teach First is associated with teacher training but runs several other programmes such as Futures and Pathways). This focus can sometimes be both positive and negative. For instance, there is a perception that Teach First teachers are on a fast track to headship and therefore do not focus on the craft of the classroom and mastering that before moving on. We do call our programme a leadership-development programme. Many of our teachers do move into positions of leadership relatively quickly. The issue with leadership is that everyone has their own view of what it means and if this is negative, it can lead to negative perceptions of any programme labelled as such. Countless studies have emphasised the importance of school leadership, alongside the expertise of the teacher, as a key determinant of pupils' success. This is not in doubt. What is more difficult to discern, however, is the type of leadership required to bring about this change. One has only to look at the burgeoning shelf of leadership manuals to see that the how of leadership is both contentious and hard to achieve.

At its simplest we see leadership at three levels: in the classroom, in the school and in the community or system. At first, participants focus on their classroom. They are leading their pupils. Some might contend that this is simply good teaching and this is to some extent true. Our focus on leadership has developed over time as we better understand the importance of making research-informed decisions in education and we have applied this rigour to leadership. We know that strong leadership in education is vital and yet the research base is patchy to say the least. The way we see leadership in relation to the programme has grown and developed over the years. This has happened in two main ways. Firstly, the extent to which leadership is domain-specific. Between 2003 and 2006, leadership content was quite distinct from teaching and learning content. The inputs were mainly from leaders in the corporate world, discussing business approaches to problems. Many participants valued the honesty of corporate leaders saying when they got things wrong, it helped them cope a little better that others made mistakes too. We also ran short programmes at business schools for our teachers. Some of our teachers valued these and found them interesting, others found it difficult to implement in their schools and so they had less relevance and applicability. In the new programme, leadership is inextricably linked to what we know about teaching and learning. We articulate this through a conceptual framework, which includes elements like 'knowledge of your pupils and their context' and an understanding of cognitive bias. Our use of generic leadership texts has therefore diminished. There are many leadership books (and many have considerable merit), but they often rely on interviews or reflections and the building of a framework around what worked for circumstances at the time, therefore limiting their transferability.

Secondly, we better understand the role that coaching plays in developing leadership. In the most recent iteration of our programme, this role belongs to our participant development leads and is backed up by a Participant Development Framework, which outlines actions in the three domains of the programme – teaching and learning, leadership and movement – and sets out the expected progress a participant can and should make in these areas. The expert way in which the participant development lead interacts with participants via the content across the three domains of the programme is a critical and unique element of the programme.

Movement

Teach First's focus on movement is driven by the understanding that we cannot make the difference we want to see alone; we need to work together across the system and mobilise our efforts towards helping schools close gaps for their most vulnerable children. The movement strand of the curriculum ensures participants see themselves as part of a network which they can both benefit from and contribute to. Whilst it can seem a nebulous term, movement has become an ever more important part of our programme, as we fully comprehend the scale of the challenge ahead of us and the importance of networks and partnerships across the system in its resolution.

Our new model

Interestingly, the thinking for our new model had begun before our most recent successful Ofsted. National data suggested that as a system we were still no closer to every child going to a good school that would provide them with the best chances in life, and it was this that drove the changes to our new programme. One could say that ITE cannot solve the issues of some children not doing as well in education related to background, but if we go back to the original idea that the difference can be made by teachers in classrooms, supported by school leaders in a conducive policy environment, then ITE is one of the largest levers that the system has. We wanted to use the two-year time frame (a relative luxury in comparison to other providers with one-year programmes) to ensure a smoother path and a more intentional trajectory to teachers being research-informed professionals, which they bring to bear on pupil learning and so, amongst other things, we introduced an advanced PGDE with 120 master's-level credits.

There are five key elements upon which the new programme rests. Firstly, through our own research, it was clear that there were a few foundational aspects of teaching that needed to be mastered to enable rapid development and unlock further and deeper development of practice. These were unsurprisingly planning, assessment, teaching and classroom management. We have termed these the 'Gatekeeper' skills, because not being able to do them well early on prevents any real success in the classroom later. This brings us to the second component, which ensures participants quickly develop and consolidate understanding in each Gatekeeper area: practice.

Practice has been heavily associated with Doug Lemov. As it has become more popular in England, there has been debate of the positives and negatives of it. For us, this work codifies what great teachers have done for years, but found it very difficult to explain for a novice to enact with precision. It focusses on the essential element of rehearsing how to be a teacher before you do it with pupils. Elements of rehearsal are common across a range of professions and, given the importance of our young people, it is even more important for our teachers. At its worst, practice could lead to nothing more than a technician applying a technique which can be very successful under a precise context but less so when the context changes, or becomes unpredictable.

This is where the third aspect of our new model comes in – research informed rigour, which infuses all aspects of the programme, enabling participants to connect robust theory to their practice. If the work in the classroom can be linked more closely to research that informs or indeed challenges it, then we see the development of professionals who can support pupils to high achievement, regardless of context or changes. By being research-informed, teachers can approach a changing or new context with confidence and calmness. They are more likely to ask and answer the right questions to enable their own development and that of pupils. In the programme, this is done through a series of module assignments. These constitute significant academic work at level 7, or master's level, yet are deeply rooted, informed by and have implications for the classroom. The first assignment focusses on our teachers building an emerging philosophy of teaching. Whilst this can sound purely academic, it aims to solve a practical issue for our teachers. Novice teachers can, especially in early practice, struggle to know why they are doing what they are doing, and how to make the best decision for pupils in a given moment. ITE focusses a great deal on teaching great lessons. This assignment takes that further, focussing on the development of a mental model of teaching, guided by a rich knowledge of pupils, context and personal values, alongside an exploration of the way evidence, experience and bias can all influence, or impact upon, teaching and learning.

The fourth component is the curriculum sequence. Our SI is now five weeks rather than six, but we have several conference weekends and days across the two years as well as a growing blended learning offer to support the programme. This prevents the need for a front loading of the curriculum, which was problematic when the SI was the main input. Whilst sequencing of major aspects is common across ITE, such as planning before assessment, we look at this at a more granular basis and are recognising that separating some of the macro elements from each other (such as planning and assessment) can lead to more issues than it resolves.

The fifth component, alongside the curriculum, is the work of those supporting our teachers. When all are aligned and clear on their unique contribution, this has the potential to be a very powerful support model. Deans for Impact, in their digital publication *Building Blocks*, suggest that, whilst difficult to achieve, alignment is essential for rapid teacher development and impact. We have reduced our support model to three principal roles, the school mentor, the university subject/phase tutor and the participant development lead. Each has a unique input and that unique contribution needs to be orchestrated across the two years. This orchestration is led by the participant development lead, with the subject/phase tutor providing the key academic subject input to inform practice and the subject mentor marrying that with subject development in context.

Summary

It is too early to fully evaluate whether these more significant changes we have made in 2017 have been successful. However, we are confident in the methodology because it is underpinned by a research-informed approach and has been more rigorously tested internally and by our partners than ever before. We are following the cohort closely to gauge what is working, and so that we can share more widely with the sector. Whilst none of this is definitive, we think that sharing ideas and approaches and the inevitable challenge and support will lead to system improvement. In the same vein, Teach First has certainly benefited from innovations across the sector as well as from high-performing countries across the world.

Our hybrid role has given us a unique opportunity to engage with universities and schools, to discuss the merits of different innovations, share successes and failures as well as genuinely debate over these areas. We all need to work within the system, to support and drive the system where it could do even better. Where we assume we are powerless to change a system, this will lead to more of the same. If we can provide evidence that certain innovations or methodologies bring success, then the system will adopt it, if it marries research and practice. One without the other will not mean ease of transfer and applicability. Pupils across the country and across the world deserve the best developed teachers possible and we are continually developing and changing our approach to ensure that we contribute to this. We have not yet succeeded in our vision, but only by constantly challenging ourselves to do better will we achieve it, both for Teach First schools and across the system.

Participant perspective: Jennifer Parker (2015 recruit)

I remember the first time I came across Teach First – it was at a careers expo during my first year of university. I walked straight past their stall, avoiding eye contact with their bouncy recruiters – I'd already ruled it out after seeing the word 'leadership' on their banner. *That wasn't for me*, I'd thought, *I'm not a leader*.

Five years later, with a degree and a master's under my belt, I found myself drifting. I was living in Australia, enjoying the sea and the sun but lacking a deeper sense of purpose. I joined Rotaract, an international community club, and was sponsored to go on a residential leadership course. On the final night, after I'd delivered a *Dragon's Den* style presentation, a man named John came over and told me in a whispered voice, *You have great leadership potential, Heather. Make sure you put it to good use*.

The next day, I looked up Teach First. The more I read – about child poverty in the UK, the unfairness of the English education system and their mission to end educational inequality – the more I knew this was what I needed to do.

A few months later, I returned to England to begin the SI – six weeks of intensive training. Though there's no denying that the notion of being ready to teach in a matter of weeks felt slightly ludicrous, I embraced the challenge and soaked up as many teaching theories, tips and *Teach like a champion* techniques as I could. By the end of it, I still didn't feel ready to be a 'real' teacher, but then perhaps you never can feel 100 per cent ready to do something you've never done before.

September soon arrived, and I found myself stood at the front of a secondary school classroom in Bristol, with 30 young faces looking inquisitively at me – their new English teacher. They didn't seem to notice that I was new to this, though, nor that I wasn't entirely sure what I was supposed to be doing. On the contrary, I think *they* believed I was a teacher even more than I did. That's one of the benefits of the Teach First route, I think; being the main classroom teacher. I've heard many times that for PGCE students, one of their greatest challenges is trying to establish themselves as a teacher with pupils who view them as merely a 'trainee'. Of course, being the main classroom teacher has its challenges, too, the biggest one being that for this year of their education, these children are relying on you, *and you alone*, to make progress in your subject or phase. I was even given a Year 11 class, for whom this would be their final year at secondary school.

Letting them down wasn't an option.

Being on a 70 per cent timetable from day one is a tall order and led me to working long days. Though I didn't notice it at first, this began to take a toll on my wellbeing. Over the summer, I reassessed my work–life balance and made some big changes to how I'd work in my second year of teaching. Though my books weren't always perfectly marked, and my lessons no longer had jazzy slides, I got my zest for life back – and I believe I was a better teacher for it, too.

Returning in year two, I felt like a very different teacher to the one who'd stood at the front of the very same classroom just one year before. I felt at ease with a room full of children looking to me for direction and couldn't wait to meet my new classes – I had such grand plans for them, and this time I felt like I knew how we were going to get there.

My second year of teaching was a breeze by comparison to the first – knowing the pupils, the school's policies and the curriculum you're teaching really helps – but one thing I did miss was the incredible support and professional development I'd become accustomed to in my first year. I'd got used to having my mentor regularly drop into my lessons to do some live coaching; to my university professors sharing their expertise on how to bring my subject to life; and to Teach First's inspiring conference days on teaching, learning and leadership. I even missed the essays and having access to academic journals. This is mitigated now by the new PGDE programme, which is master's level and spans the two full years of the programme, plus the Chartered College of Teaching now enables all teachers to have access to journals.

Throughout the two years, I found that as a teacher you spend most of your time either by yourself or with a class of pupils, but rarely with other adults, and this can sometimes feel quite isolating. For me, having a fellow Teach First participant down the corridor who I could go and chat with really helped, as did remembering the 55 other participants in the south west doing the same thing as me. Add to that 1,400 participants in my cohort, plus over 10,000 ambassadors across England and Wales, and I'd remember that I'm not alone. I'm part of something much bigger than myself – I'm part of a movement of social change, and while no one person can do it alone, together I do believe we will make educational inequality a thing of the past. With Teach First, I'd found my purpose.

Conclusion

Teach First has engaged with the existing system and entered into partnership with schools and HE. There has been ongoing involvement of HE since the beginning of Teach First. There is an emphasis on research-led teaching and the development of a particular approach to teaching. No one can doubt that Teach First has been a success in terms of numbers and the wider profile it has generated. The objective as citied in the participant account above, to 'make educational inequality a thing of the past', would be supported by any rational person and it is clear from the two accounts that there is a strong commitment to achieve this. However, there are strong supporters of the initiative and there are also those who consider that it has had little impact on the wider teaching profession (see for example Leaton-Gray and Whitty, 2010). We have also recorded some criticism of the limited teaching approaches adopted by Teach First participants in Chapter 8. It is often difficult to reconcile the differing views of Teach First and there is a need for further research work on it, given their desire to change the system and their ongoing growth and importance within the system.

10
CONCLUSION

Previous chapters have described a range of key initiatives and interventions that were introduced to manage initial teacher education in England. It has been acknowledged that there have been, and continue to be, long-standing and complex debates about how teachers should be educated, how the training should be managed and by whom, and how higher education institutions (HEIs) and schools should work together to achieve the goal of recruiting the best teachers while providing them with high-quality training (Childs, 2013).

References have been made to legislation and policy initiatives which have helped to shape the form and nature of initial teacher education, to the introduction of government activities at 'arm's length' through quangos such as the Teacher Training Agency (TTA) and Ofsted, and the contributions of policy reviews and special reports (for example, the Carter Review, the Schools White Paper, The Importance of Teaching (DfE, 2010), the Conservative Government White Paper: Educational Excellence Everywhere (DfE, 2016a)). The contributions of secretaries of state, with their own political and idiosyncratic beliefs about teacher education (for example, Clarke and Baker in the early 1990s and Gove in more recent times) have all been highlighted. At the same time, the consensus about the direction of change with regard to teacher education, held by Conservative, Labour and the Coalition governments since the 1990s, was identified. Attention has been given to different governments' reform agendas, particularly with regard to the policy requirements, regulation and governance of initial teacher training (ITT) in the context of the reform of, and constant restructuring of, the whole education system in England.

There have been clear contradictions in certain aspects of teacher training policy with regard to the control from government. For example, Childs (2013: 323) summarises these issues succinctly when she writes: 'the policy trajectory from the late 1970s, no matter what the political make-up of the government, has been to increase freedom, choice and diversity in teacher education in order to drive up standards in true neoliberal style'.

At the same time, previous chapters have also suggested that the ITT sector in England has been subject, in recent times, to increasing levels of centralisation, monitoring and accountability (McNamara et al., 2017), while the education sector itself has become more fragmented and diverse than in any other period since the Second World War.

Policy changes in the sector have been numerous, and previous chapters have referred for example to key initiatives since the nineteenth century. In more recent times there has been a raft of interventions affecting profoundly such issues as new training routes, the favoured models of teaching and teacher preparation, the notion of partnership and the changing teacher educator's professional roles and identities.

The one reform agenda that has been most radical and critical since the 1990s has been the move towards school-led ITT, and there has been an increase in the intensity of change in the years since the emergence of the Coalition government. It is important not to forget that within teacher education as a whole in England today, there are many strengths that should be highlighted in any discussion about improving the system. For example, reference should be made to the following characteristics:

- partnerships between schools and universities are highly developed;
- there is a relatively robust quality-assurance system in place which is recognised internationally;
- qualified teacher status is awarded only after a process of rigorous assessment;
- selection to ITT programmes is, on the whole, rigorous;
- there is a culture of continuous quality improvement in certain aspects of provision, for example, in partnership work;
- the HEI–school provision ensures that there are opportunities for engagement with recent and relevant research.

This chapter will comment on the following issues which have been identified in previous chapters as key to discussion and debate about initial teacher education and training:

- The ways in which the nature of teacher education has changed as HE institutions have had to adapt to a range of different models introduced by government and its agencies.
- The changing role of higher education (HE) and the growing importance of schools in the training of teachers.
- The roles of key government organisations which have played a key role in changing the landscape of teacher education in England in the period under review. Particular reference is made to the TTA and its subsequent reincarnations and Ofsted.

- The lessons that can be learned from examining the different approaches to teacher education in systems in international contexts.
- The future role of HE in ITT.

Teacher education and changing government models

As has been described in previous chapters, individuals who enter ITT each year in England can choose from several routes, although the main ones are either school-centred, such as School Direct and Teach First, or university-led, such as PGCE courses. The policy of recent governments in England has signalled the move towards 'an increasingly school-led ITT system' (DfE, 2016b: 28). The sector has therefore seen a trend whereby an increasing proportion of trainees, approximately 30,000 each year, enter ITT through school-led routes. The percentages for those starting training in 2015/16 were as follows:

- university-led (undergraduate) 16%
- university-led (post-graduate) 41%
- School Direct – fee (post-graduate) 21%
- School Direct – salaried (post-graduate) 10%
- School-centred ITT (post-graduate) 7%
- Teach First 5%.

Within the university-led approach and the school-led approach, a number of different training routes are available for both undergraduates and graduates, and these have been described and discussed in earlier chapters. It is not surprising that the Education Committee in their report on the recruitment and retention of teachers noted that the 'number of different routes into teaching are not always understood by applicants and can be confusing' (2017: 9–10).

Inevitably, the focus on school-led routes has led some HEIs to review the sustainability of their provision. Government reactions have been to emphasise the history of successful collaboration between HEIs and schools, for example in School Direct courses, and to state that school-led systems do not exclude universities (Hansard, 2015). At the same time, a National Audit Office report (2016), commented that while there was an increase in the supply of school-led training, HEIs were being kept in the market.

As well as HEIs having to review their roles in relation to their work with schools, the changing teacher training landscape has also led to a situation where university-based and school-based educators have had to reconsider their roles and identities, in order to adapt to continuously shifting contexts.

Brown et al. (2014: 20), in their comprehensive report on School Direct, suggest that 'the new model is changing the position of schools to operate like consumers and for universities', as one person interviewed commented, to act like 'gas' providers.

Changes in power relationships between schools and HEIs, fuelled by increased competition introduced by governments, appear to have tipped the balance of power towards the former. It seems therefore inevitable that historical partnership arrangements will be continuously altered and reshaped, and issues such as continuing professional development and the teaching of subject knowledge will allow schools the opportunity to take on increasing responsibilities.

Both HEIs and schools will need to review these changing responsibilities, but with recognition of their often long-established relationships and the expertise that both parties have developed over the years. The changing context in the relationships between universities and schools have tested the lines of accountability between the two stakeholders, which raises the issue of which of the two is likely to be most affected by quality-assurance systems and procedures, such as Ofsted. This point is discussed later in the chapter, as is the importance of the outcomes of 'high-stakes' inspection regimes, for both universities and schools.

This is not to say that schools have been unwilling to take advantage of the opportunities and benefits of securing greater responsibility for managing teacher training. It could be argued that the more strategically minded school leaders saw opportunities in the confused landscape caused by so many policy changes, particularly where responsibilities were not clearly demarcated.

The importance of the power relationship between schools and universities has been referred to in previous chapters. Inevitably, both groups had to develop more strategically appropriate responses in their approaches to partnership working, and it has been argued that universities, in practice, were forced to play a more strategic negotiating role (Brown et al., 2014).

Another key issue related to the shifting balance of power that both universities and schools have had to confront is the challenge to the roles of teacher educators and their contributions to teacher education in an ever changing landscape. Prior to 1979, the role and remit of university teacher educators had been relatively well defined and accepted by governments, universities and schools. In more recent times, the distinctive role of university teacher educators has been subject to major changes and, consequently, the boundaries between universities and schools have become blurred. It seems possible that in the future there will be more school-based teacher educators.

Indeed, Childs (2013: 319) suggests that successive governments have 'seriously undermined and eroded the work of teacher educators' in the changing teacher education landscape. The 'traditional' roles of university teacher educators have changed, from those teaching subjects such as philosophy, psychology, history and sociology, and subject studies specialists and curriculum methods experts, to staff focussed almost entirely on the latter areas, and in mentoring and coaching trainees.

As schools have become more significant partners, schoolteachers have had the opportunity themselves to become school-based teacher educators. There is, implicit in this movement, the government's agenda that teacher educators should emerge from a process that privileges on-the-job training and sees teaching as a craft-centred profession – hence the possible demise of other university teacher education institutions as has been seen in the last few years.

In England, initiatives such as the development of teaching schools and the emerging networks of academic chains which provide their own continuing professional development programmes might further weaken the ways in which universities relate to teacher training. Universities might be asked only to provide accreditation for teacher training courses – indeed, one teaching school alliance has already negotiated awarding master's-level credits for the courses that it offers.

However, it could be argued that some universities have taken the initiative to be proactive in the current context and are therefore experimenting with different models. In contrast, some of the other departments we spoke to were experimenting with a range of different models in order to meet the changing demands by schools. The review by Brown et al. (2014) highlights one example of a large teaching school alliance where all training is carried out by a university-based teacher educator and a school-based teacher educator on the school site.

Government policy in recent years has appeared to encourage alternatives to what has been seen by them as university hegemony over teacher education. It would be naïve to believe that future governments will push back from the policies and practices that have already been enacted. Nevertheless, there are signs that the provision of different pathways into teaching can stimulate innovation and can help to improve the quality of new programmes, as long as that quality is maintained and regularly reviewed. It is always useful to take the opportunity to view what is happening in other systems and, as Zeichner (2014) notes, high-performing countries all appear to be enthusiastic about preserving and strengthening the role of colleges and universities in the preparation of a professional teaching force – an issue that will be discussed later in this chapter.

HE, schools and the changing nature of teacher education

There has been discussion in previous chapters of the fact that historically in England, ITT has been carried out by HEIs. Indeed, they have a long-standing record of providing both on-the-job practical experience and in schools and in university they have developed in-depth subject and pedagogical knowledge to trainees. Over the years, therefore, HEIs have amassed considerable levels of expertise in teacher education and training. Universities UK reports that in 2010–12, there were 73 HEIs providing ITT courses in England, and about 80 per cent of training places were allocated directly to participating universities (2014: 5).

In recent years, and particularly with the introduction of the School Direct training route, HEIs have had to react to a government ambition whereby schools lead on the recruitment and training of teachers. The rate and pace of change, especially since the 2011 white paper, has affected some HEIs more than others. HEIs have had to deal with changes in the number of student places allocated to them, with all of the resource implications following from this, and they have had to review how they engage with schools. Inevitably, the changing situation has forced some HEIs to ask questions about their long-term commitment and ability, to deliver ITT courses in specific subject areas, or even in the overall provision of ITT.

The shift towards more school-based provision, away from a university setting, raises several key concerns. Furlong et al. (2009) refer to the marginalisation of the university in the future preparation of teachers.

The role of the TTA, HEIs and government

Previous chapters have identified and discussed the various organisations that governments have established to manage teacher education in the post-war period. All governments in the period reviewed have made comprehensive use of these organisations. References have been made to, for example, CATE, Mote 1 and Mote 2, and the various configurations of the TTA. The latter has undergone several configurations from its inception in 1994, to become the Training and Development Agency in 2005, the Teaching Agency in 2012 and the National College for Teaching and Leadership (NCTL) in 2013. In November 2017, the Department for Education announced that the NCTL will close from April 2018, with its teacher-recruitment functions merged into the Department for Education. A new executive agency, the Teaching Regulation Agency, will take on the NCTL's functions relating to regulation of the teaching profession.

It should be noted that since 1944, and prior to the introduction of Ofsted, HMI was largely responsible, as Lee and Fitz (1997: 41) point out, for: 'conducting Inspection largely of schools, writing confidential reports and, crucially, reflecting the state of the system back to government. Throughout its history, the inspectorate was a cohesive and close-knit body.'

It has been argued that the creation of the TTA (1995) 'signalled a paradigm shift in relationships between HEIs, LEAs [local education authorities] and central government, and consolidated the move to a much greater degree of central control in both initial teacher training and in CPD [continuing professional development]' (Bates et al., 1999: 324). The writers focus on the importance of the issue of control by government of ITT, a theme which has been emphasised many times in the previous chapters, and one which is central in any discussion of the assessment of the roles of the various stakeholders with legitimate interests in initial teacher education, particularly that of HE as a key stakeholder.

Changing relationships between central government, its agencies and stakeholders have been consistent challenges to a 'rationale' and consensual approach to teacher education, and have affected the spirit of partnership that was prevalent before the 1980s. The ways in which different countries approach this relationship will be discussed later.

Inspection of teacher education in England and inspection in international contexts

It has been pointed out in Chapter 4 that in England Ofsted is responsible for inspecting all providers of ITT programmes leading to qualified teacher status, and has been since 1995, when it began to carry out inspections on behalf of the TTA. Prior to this, inspection of ITT had been carried out by HMI on behalf of the Department of Education and Science, under a concordat agreed between HMI and the universities.

Ofsted's mission has remained relatively stable over the last 25 years and, despite some structural upheaval, it has become a driver of change and, some might argue, a force for good (Morris, 2013).

Clearly, the outcomes of Ofsted inspections are of crucial importance to HEIs and to schools. A study by Brown et al. (2014) of the School Direct initiative refers to the impact of Ofsted judgements, particularly the way in which these can affect the HEI's standing in the local market with regard to provision and competition with other 'providers'. Thus, in England, whether a university education department is allocated any ITT depends on their inspection ratings. Consequently, receiving an 'outstanding' from Ofsted is a coveted award.

Internationally, ITT is itself subject to critical scrutiny as countries and systems strive to improve the quality of their provision. For example, Whitby (2010), in her report on inspection practices in a range of countries with developed education systems, comments that as school decentralisation becomes increasingly widespread internationally, 'school inspection systems are assuming key importance in ensuring quality provision for all' (2010: 3).

International comparisons also provide the opportunity to identify similarities and differences between England and the United Kingdom (UK) and other systems, in order to consider what can be learned from perceived differences, and how they might be used to inform the shape of future inspections. Inevitably when making comparisons, it is necessary to acknowledge the powerful political, historical, social and economic factors that influence the judgements made by the inspectors.

Evidence suggests that the importance of inspection of teacher training between countries can be described as heterogeneous. For example, Governance of Education Trajectories in Europe carried out a comparative analysis of the organisation of teacher training in eight European countries (Cramer et al., 2013). There were inspections of the ITT systems in each country, with a focus on education policy, school practice, programme content and relationships with other education actors. The research was based on the use of three major sources: a survey of institutions, document analysis and expert interviews. There are clear differences in the ways in which inspection is placed in the different countries. In Slovenia, France and Poland, inspection appears to have little importance. In the UK and in Germany, its importance is judged to be moderate, while in Finland, the Netherlands and Italy, inspection seems to carry a very high value.

GOETE's reporting that inspection of ITT in the UK is judged as 'moderate' is interesting, given the high stakes attached to the outcomes of Ofsted inspections in England. It could be assumed that not all providers, particularly HEIs in England, would offer a moderate judgement of the importance of inspection by Ofsted. The latter has had what might be described as a 'chequered history' in terms of its relations with HEIs. There have been instances, in England at least, where the quality, impartiality and effectiveness of Ofsted inspections and inspectors has been called into account (see for example Campbell and Husbands, 2000 and UCET, 2013). The latter organisation, UCET (The Universities Council for the Education of Teachers) which is the national forum for the discussion of matters relating to the education of teachers and professional educators in the university sector, accused Ofsted of being 'overtly political' and seeking to 'justify government policy' on ITT as recently as 2013.

However, recent Ofsted inspections of teacher training annual reports, published in 2017, provide valuable insights into the health of school-led and university-led partnerships in England. The overall quality of training was described by Ofsted as high in both school-led and university-led partnerships. Ninety-nine per cent of university-led partnerships and 100 per cent of school-led partnerships were judged to be 'good' or 'outstanding' after their most recent inspection.

More generally in terms of inspection, there are also differences in the ways in which other countries appear to adopt alternative approaches to governing education, while hoping for similar outcomes. For example, in Sweden there is a strong focus on regulation and compliance with regard to inspection, while in Scotland there is greater reliance on self-evaluation. Countries differ in how much they use 'punitive' methods or more developmental ones (Germany). In Austria and Switzerland, a 'non-punitive' approach, using persuasion, feedback and support, is favoured.

This raises questions about the recruitment and training of the inspectorate in different systems. It is interesting to note that Sweden has changed its policy of recruiting inspectors from an education background, to a policy emphasising the recruitment of legal professionals and those with a background in research and proven investigative skills.

The future role of HEIs in teacher education

The main issues here concern the relative strengths of the various stakeholders in the negotiating and brokering that takes place as policy directions are brought into play. A glance at the history of the relationship between HE and governments in the UK in the post-war period shows the gradual erosion of the former's power, and the increasing intention and capacity of government to take the lead in steering policy direction.

If we abandon the idea that HE has a fundamental role in the initial training of teachers, a new generation of teachers will teach future generations of children without having any understanding of educational theory. New teachers will have little idea what education means. The consequences will be entirely negative and hard to reverse.

There are several key questions that HEIs, government and other stakeholders need to consider in determining the contribution of HEIs to initial teacher education in England in the foreseeable future.

- HEIs could be given a more substantial role in initial teacher education.
- The status quo could be maintained.
- HEIs could be written out of the picture, as initial teacher education is offered to other organisations such as quangos. It has been questioned by some that the increasing focus on school-led routes could bring into question the sustainability of some university-centred provision. For example, the Open University, Bath Spa University and Anglia Ruskin University have all recently withdrawn some of their teacher training provision (Universities UK, 2014).
- Government could take on an even more direct 'hands-on' approach by encouraging opportunities for initial teacher education to become 'privatised', by increasing deregulation and by championing the increase of unqualified teachers, for example in academies, free schools and public schools.

Future roles for HE in teacher education: learning from international models

Reference has been made several times in this book to the increase in competition in international comparative testing and educational achievement, which inevitably has had a direct impact on the conceptions of teacher quality and hence teacher education, in different contexts (Barber and Moushed, 2007; Morris, 2012).

Conroy et al. (2013: 1) refer to the 're-positioning of teacher education that has taken place over the last three decades' and to the focus on the reform of school systems and the redesign of teacher education. The authors, in a discussion of the work of Sahlberg, speak of 'a global education reform movement that has promoted the standardization of education, corporate management and test-based accountability policies' (Conroy et al., 2013: 2), all of which impact to some extent on the initial preparation and training of teachers.

It is recognised that countries and systems face different challenges in ITT and the design of teacher education, training and development has to respond to the specific needs of each system. As Mussett indicates, 'research shows that the most effective way to raise educational quality is to modify initial teacher education and recruitment, and to develop the means to train teachers that are already in service ' (2010: 3).

However, a word of caution is necessary when comparisons are being made across international systems. For example, Morris (2012), in a detailed analysis of the 2010 white paper, criticises the 'evidence-based' approach to policy making where politicians in England have used policy borrowing to 'select and project their own agendas' (2012: 105). The practice of looking across national borders for educational inspiration has existed for some time (Phillips and Schweisfurth, 2006) and has been used to 'identify, initiate and legitimise education reform in order to secure a competitive edge' (Chung, 2016: 214).

There has been a growing tendency for policy makers and key players to cherry-pick evidence that supports any chosen policy direction and justifies favoured ideas and actions. Countries such as Finland, Canada and Singapore have been identified as 'role models', but obviously what works well in one country or system will not necessarily work in another.

What is not in doubt is the fact that the quality of teaching is recognised as being a significant influencing factor when analysing school achievement and outcomes. Therefore, the ways in which teachers are educated and trained has become an important factor when comparisons are made between different countries and systems. For example, it has been suggested by Browne and Reid (2012) that there are contrasting models between, for example, England and those countries in the European Teacher Education Area. These models, it is argued, represent very different conceptions of teacher training.

The authors suggest that teacher education in England has been gradually transferred from its traditional home within the academy to school-led training. This is in stark contrast to the European model, which is also concerned with improving teacher quality but prefers to maintain support for academic study, with an emphasis on pedagogy taught from the beginning of teacher-education programmes and with, compared to England, a relatively short period spent in schools (Browne and Reid, 2012).

This move towards a school-led system can also be contrasted with international trends in many high-performing school systems, where universities are still placed at the centre of ITT provision. It might be argued that policies in England appear to 'fly in the face' of best practice internationally. However, it is essential to remember that what has been asserted, often in policy documents from government, in the form of the 'what works' rhetoric about the success of high-performing nations or systems, should be treated with caution.

Nevertheless, there are opportunities to review the practices of other systems in a systematic and objective way – if this is at all possible. To illustrate these points a number of ITT systems in high-performing nations are now highlighted.

A report by Universities UK (2014) refers to the systems in Finland, South Korea and Singapore, which are all high-performing systems in international comparisons of student achievement. It is clear that the move towards a school-led system in England is in stark contrast to the approach to ITT provision in those countries. For example, in Finland, teacher education was moved in the 1970s from teacher training colleges into universities.

Chapter 6 outlined the Finnish system, where recruitment to ITT is highly selective and all teachers are required to hold a master's degree. There is an emphasis on the importance of pedagogical content and a commitment to provide trainees in all sectors with research skills. The Finnish system provides evidence of a commitment to giving recognition and support to teachers, in allowing them to make professional judgements about their evidence-based practice, based on the skills and expertise developed in their ITT programmes. Chung (2016), in a recent article, argues that the Finnish model of teacher education has been borrowed uncritically by UK policy makers. Issues such as the differing philosophies of teacher preparation between Finland and England have not been assimilated by English policy makers and, as Chung points out, 'the Finnish teacher education model does not fit within the teacher "training" viewpoint of England' (Chung, 2016: 207), or education policies and approaches to education.

The situation in South Korea, another high-performing system, is similar to that in Finland in some respects. For instance, teacher education takes place within dedicated teachers' colleges or in the departments of education in universities.

In Singapore the situation is rather different because there is only one teacher training institution: the National Institute of Education at the Nanyang Technological University. The government in Singapore has made significant improvements since recognising a low point in teacher training in the 1980s. The focus in all courses relating to initial teacher education and training at the institute is on pedagogy and instruction in the craft of teaching.

Concluding comments

Initial teacher education, in the international context, has maintained a sharp focus on attracting, preparing and retaining quality teachers, hence the debate and discussion on the quality of the teaching profession.

Decision makers will need to evaluate key learning from the ways in which initial teacher education has developed in the recent past, in order to present coherent, appropriate and effective policies to inform future practice. In an ideal world, these policies will be evidence-based and, as well as considering the English experiences, will look at practice in other systems. In the past, too often policy has been driven by ideological considerations. This has been shown to be the case in all the historical periods discussed in previous chapters, whether there have been Labour, Conservative or Coalition governments, although in the post-war period between 1945 and the early 1970s, education was not 'high on the agenda' and there was a period of relative consensus between Labour and Conservative governments (Abbott et al., 2013).

Are there likely to be any radical changes to current provision?

It can be argued that funding of initial teacher education will have its challenges, particularly in a relatively unknown future dominated by the new post-referendum position of the UK in Europe. It might be safely assumed that there will be no radical shifts in provision, that governments will proceed with a relatively cautious approach and that the emphasis will be on cost-effective provision.

Much of the evidence relating to educational reform in general can be described as incremental and characterised by an unquestioning endorsement of the status quo, a lack of imagination and a lack of critique of current trends (Codd et al., 2013).

In England, there appears to have been a reluctance to learn from past policy. Cater (2017: 40) writes that: 'There is a frustrating reluctance to take lessons from past policy, and particularly where that policy emanated from a government of a different political colour'.

The government stated in a debate in the House of Lords (2015: 37) that 'a school-led system does not mean a university excluded system', and emphasised the collaboration between schools and universities in school-led courses, namely School Direct. The government and NCTL appear to be in favour of increasing the supply of school-led training while keeping universities in the market. These issues have been commented upon recently by Howson, who, in a presentation on ITE suggested: 'The various routes into teaching have been undergoing a fundamental politically driven change from a higher education based system to a school-led system. This change has occurred as the economy has shifted from recession into a period of growth' (Howson, 2015).

There are interesting lessons to be learnt from other systems, particularly those that have continued to be successful in international comparisons.

However, there may be reasons to be optimistic at the time of writing, as there appears to be a greater emphasis on partnership-based approaches with more interest in the value and importance of research-informed practice, signalling a move away from a school-led agenda.

If there is a genuine desire to create a world-class system of teacher education in England then there is a need for substantial investment in the continuing professional development of teachers, with a focus on the strategic direction for the pattern of teacher education provision in future years.

Evidence from home and from international systems suggests that there needs to be a focus on research activities, and a need for master's level and doctoral studies, so that teachers enter schools with the skills and abilities to be key players in curriculum development, in research and in the leadership of teaching and learning. Past experience and evidence from that experience, demonstrates that universities have the power and knowledge to lead in the intellectual underpinning necessary for success in each of these key attributes highlighted above. When looking to the future, albeit with a focussed gaze at the recent past, it is important to recognise the complexity of the issues involved in the quest for a world-class system of teacher education in England.

REFERENCES

Abbott, I. (2008) *Celebrating 60 Years of Teacher Training*. Warwick: University of Warwick.
Abbott, I. (2015) Politics and Education Policy into Practice: Conversations with Former Secretaries of State. *Journal of Educational Administration and Leadership*, Vol. 47, No. 4, 334–349.
Abbott, I., Rathbone, M. and Whitehead, P. (2013) *Education Policy*. London: SAGE.
Alexander, R. (ed.) (2010) *Children, Their World, Their Education: Final Report and Recommendations of the Cambridge Primary Education Review*. London: Routledge.
Alexander, R., RoseJ. and Woodhead, C. (1992) *Curriculum Organisation and Classroom Practice in Primary Schools*. London: Department of Education and Science.
Allen, R. and Allnutt, J. (2017) The Impact of Teach First on Pupil Attainment at Age 16. *British Educational Research Journal*, Vol. 43, No. 4, 627–646.
Baker, K. (1993) *The Turbulent Years: My Life in Politics*. London: Faber & Faber.
Ball, S. (1994) *Education Reform: A Critical and Post Structural Approach*. Buckingham: Open University Press.
Ball, S. (2003a) *Class Strategies and the Education Market*. London: Routledge/Falmer.
Ball, S. (2003b) The Teacher's Soul and the Terrors of Performativity. *Journal of Education Policy*, 18(2), 215–228.
Ball, S. (2008) *The Education Debate*. Bristol: Policy Press.
Barber, M. and Moushed, M. (2007) How the World's Best-Performing Systems Come out on Top. www.smhc-cpre.org/wp-content/uploads/2008/07/how-the-worlds-best-performing-school-systems-come-out-on-top-sept-072.pdf.
Bates, T., Gough, B. and Stammers, P. (1999) The Role of Central Government and Its Agencies in the Continuing Professional Development of Teachers: An Evaluation of Recent Changes in Its Financing in England. *Journal of In-Service Education*, Vol. 25, No. 2, 321–335.
BBC (2018) GCSE Results Rise despite Tougher Exams. www.bbc.co.uk/news/education.
Becher, T. (1992) Never Mind the EDU, What about CATE? The Background to Current Developments in English Teacher Education. *Australian Journal of Teacher Education*, Vol. 17, No. 2, 76–83.

Beckett, L. and Nuttall, A. (2017) A 'Usable Past' of Teacher Education in England: History in JET's Anniversary Issue. *Journal of Education of Teaching*, Vol. 43, No. 5, 616–627.

Bennett, N. (1976) *Teaching Styles and Pupil Progress*. Cambridge, MA: Harvard University Press.

Bennett, N. (1987) Changing Perspectives on Teaching and Learning Processes in the Post-Plowden Era. *Oxford Education Review*, Vol. 13, No. 1, 67–77.

BERA-RSA (2014) Research and the Teaching Profession: Building the Capacity for a Self-Improving Education System. Final Report of the BERA-RSA Inquiry.

Bereiter, C. and Engelmann, S. (1966) *Teaching Disadvantaged Children in the Pre-School*. Engelwood Cliffs, NJ: Prentice-Hall.

Bernstein, B. (1970) Education Cannot Compensate for Society. *New Society*, Vol. 15, No. 387, 344–347.

Black, S. and YasukawaK. (2016) Research that Counts: OECD Statistics and Policy Entrepreneurs Impacting on Australian Adult Literacy and Numeracy Policy. *Research in Post-Compulsory Education*, Vol. 21, No. 3, 185–190.

Blatchford, K. and Gash, T. (2012) *Commissioning for Success*. London: Institute for Government.

Board of Education (1870) Elementary Education Act. London: HMSO.

Board of Education (1899) To Provide for the Establishment of a Board of Education for England and Wales. London: HMSO.

Board of Education (1902) The Balfour Act. London: HMSO.

Board of Education (1906) Report of the Consultative Committee upon Questions Affecting Higher Elementary Schools. London: HMSO.

Board of Education (1918) The Fisher Act. London: HMSO.

Board of Education (1933) Infant and Nursery Schools (Hadow Report). London: HMSO.

Board of Education (1938) The Spens Report. The Report of the Consultative Committee on Secondary Education. London: HMSO.

Board of Education (1943) Education Reconstruction (White Paper). London: HMSO.

Board of Education (1944) Report of Committee to Consider the Supply, Recruitment and Training of Teachers and Youth Leaders (McNair Report). London: HMSO.

Brant, J. and VincentK. (2017) Teacher Education in England: Professional Preparation in Times of Change. In Trippestad, T.A., Swennen, A. and Werler, T. (eds), *The Struggle for Teacher Education*. London: Bloomsbury.

Brighouse, T. (1991) *What Makes a Good School?*Stafford: Network Educational Press.

Brooks, V. (2006) A Quiet Revolution? The Impact of Training Schools on Initial Teacher Training Partnerships. *Journal of Education for Teaching*, Vol. 32, No. 4, 379–393.

Brown, T., Rowley, H. and Smith, K. (2014) The Beginnings of School Led Teacher Training: New Challenges for University Teacher Education. www.esri.mmu.ac.uk/resgroups/schooldirect.pdf.

Brown-Martin, G. (2014) *Learning Re-imagined*. London: Bloomsbury Academic.

Browne, E. and Reid, J. (2012) The Changing Localities of Teacher Education. *Journal of Education for Teachers*, Vol. 38, No. 4.

Burns, D. and Darling-Hammond, L. (2014) *Teaching around the World: What Can TALIS Tell Us?*Stanford, CA: Stanford Center for Opportunity Policy in Education.

Campbell, J. and Husbands, C. (2000) On the Reliability of OFSTED Inspection of Initial Teacher Training: A Case Study. *British Educational Research Journal*, Vol. 26, No. 1.

Carr, W. and Hartnett, A. (1996) *Education and the Struggle for Democracy*. Philadelphia, PA: Oxford University Press.

Carter, A. (2015) Carter Review of Initial Teacher Training (ITT). London: Department for Education.

Cater, J. (2017) Whither Teacher Education and Training? HEPI Report 95. www.hepi.ac.uk/2017/04/27/whither-teacher-education-training/.

Challinor, E.B. (1978) *The Story of St Mary's College*. Cheltenham: Challinor.

Cheesewright, P. (2008) *The University of Worcester*. London: James and James.

Chung, J. (2016) The (Mis)use of the Finnish Teacher Education Model: 'Policy-Based Evidence-Making'? *Educational Research*, Vol. 58, No. 2, 207–219.

Childs, A. (2013) The Work of Teacher Educators: An English Policy Perspective. *Journal of Education and Teaching*, Vol. 39, No. 3, 314–328.

Cholmondly, E. (1960) *The Story of Charlotte Mason 1842–1923*. Letchworth: Dent.

Codd, J.A., Brown, M., Clark, J., McPherson, J., O'Neill, H., Waitere-Ang, H. and Zepke, N. (2002) Review of Future-Focused Research on Teaching and Learning. In Snoek, M. (2013), From Splendid Isolation to Crossed Boundaries? The Futures of Teacher Education in the Light of Activity Theory. *Teacher Development*, Vol. 17, No. 3, 307–321.

Coe, R., Aloisi, C., Higgins, S. and Major, L.E. (2014) *What Makes Great Teaching? Review of the Underpinning Research*. London: Sutton Trust.

Conroy, J., Hulme, M. and Menter, I. (2013) Developing a 'Clinical' Model for Teacher Education. *Journal of Education for Teaching*. http://dx.doi.org/10.1080/02607476.2013.836339.

Cordingley, P. (2015) The Contribution of Research to Teachers' Professional Learning and Development. *Oxford Review of Education*, Vol. 41, No. 2, 234–252.

Cox, C.B. and Dyson, A.E. (eds) (1969) *Fight for Education: A Black Paper*. London: Critical Quarterly Society.

Craig, A.G. (1843) *The Philosophy of Training*. London: Cambridge University Press.

Cramer, C., Thorsten, B. and duBois-Reymond, M. (2013) Comparative Report: Teacher Training. file:///C:/Users/prwhi/Downloads/GOETE_deliverable%20no.16_Comparative%20report%20teacher%20training.pdf.

Crisp, B. (2017) An Interview with Philippa Cordingley (CUREE). *Warwick Journal of Education-Transforming Teaching*, Vol. 1, 10–11.

Crossley, M. and Sprague, T. (2012) The Policy Impact of International Data on Student Achievement: A Cautionary Note and Research Agenda. International Datasets and Comparisons in Education. *British Educational Research Association*, Vol. 119, Autumn/Winter, 22–23.

Darling-Hammond, L. (2010) *The Flat World and Education*. New York: Teachers College Press.

Darling-Hammond, L. and Rothman, R. (eds) (2011) *Teacher and Leader Effectiveness in High-Performing Education Systems*. Washington, DC: Alliance for Excellent Education and Stanford, CA: Stanford Center for Opportunity Policy in Education.

Darling-Hammond, L., Chung Wei, R. and Andree, A. (2010) *How High-Achieving Countries Develop Great Teachers*. Stanford, CA: Stanford Centre for Opportunity Policy in Education.

Davies, J. and Harrison, M. (1995) Mentors' Roles in a Primary Articled Teacher Scheme. *Mentoring and Tutoring: Partnership in Learning*, Vol. 3, No. 1, 49–56.

Davies, N. (2000) *The School Report*. London: Vintage.

DCSF (2007) The Children's Plan. London: HMSO.

DCSF (2009) Independent Review of the Primary Curriculum: Final Report. London: HMSO.

DEL (2014) Final Report of the International Review Panel on the Structure of Initial Teacher Education in Northern Ireland. www.delni.gov.uk/sites/default/files/publications/del/Structure%20of%20Initial%20Teacher%20Education%20in%20Northern%20Ireland%20Final%20Report.pdf.

Deng, Z. and Saravanan, G. (2015) PISA and High Performing Education Systems: Reflections on Preliminary Findings in the Context of Asian Knowledge Building. THF Working Paper, Working Paper Series No. 5/2015. HEAD Foundation.
DES (1959) 15 to 19: A Report of the Central Advisory Committee for Education (Crowther Report). London: HMSO.
DES (1963a) Half Our Future: A Report of the Central Advisory Council for Education (Newsome Report). London: HMSO.
DES (1963b) Higher Education: A Report of the Committee Appointed under the Chairmanship of Lord Robbins (Robbins Report). London: HMSO.
DES (1965) The Organisation of Secondary Education. Circular 10/65. London: HMSO.
DES (1967) Children and Their Primary Schools: A Report of the Central Advisory Council for Education (Plowden Report). London: HMSO.
DES (1972a) A Framework for Expansion. London: HMSO.
DES (1972b) Teacher Education and Training (James Report). London: HMSO.
DES (1973) Circular 7/73. London: HMSO.
DES (1977) Education in Schools: A Consultative Document. London: HMSO.
DES (1979) Developments in the B.Ed Course. HMI Series for Discussion 8. London: HMSO.
DES (1983) Teaching Quality. London: HMSO.
DES (1984) Circular 3/84. Initial Teacher Training: Approval of Courses. London: HMSO.
DES (1985) Better Schools. London: HMSO.
Dewey, J. (1916) *Democracy and Education: An Introduction to the Philosophy of Education*. London: Macmillan.
DfE (2010) The Importance of Teaching: Schools White Paper. London: HMSO.
DfE (2011) Training Our Next Generation of Outstanding Teachers: Implementation Plan. London: DfE.
DfE (2015) The Importance of Teaching. London: HMSO.
DfE (2016a) Education Excellence Everywhere. London: HMSO.
DfE (2016b) Initial teacher Training: Government Response to Carter Review. London: HMSO.
DfE (2016c) Schools that Work for Everyone. Government Consultation Paper, 12 September. www.gov.uk.
DfE (2017) Postgraduate Teaching Apprenticeships: Guidance for Providers and Schools. www.gov.uk.
DfE (2018a) Requesting Initial Teacher Training Places. London: DfE.
DfE (2018b) Strengthening Qualified Teacher Status and Improving Career Progression for Teachers: Government Consultation Response. https://assets.publishing.service.gov.uk/government/uploads/system/uploads/attachment_data/file/704942/Government_consultation_response_-_QTS_and_career_progression.pdf.
DfE (2018c) Teacher Workforce Statistics and Analysis: Analysis of Teacher Supply, Retention and Mobility. www.gov.uk/government/collections/teacher-workforce-statistics-and-analysis.
DfE Research Report (2012) DFE-RR243a. London: UK NARICV.
DfEE (1998) Teaching and Higher Education Act. London: HMSO.
DfEE (2000) Research into Teacher Effectiveness: A Model of Teacher Effectiveness. Hay McBer Report. London: HMSO.
DfES (1998) Circular 4/98: Teachers Meeting the Challenge of Change. London: HMSO.
DfES (2005) Education Act. London: HMSO.
DfES (2007) The Children's Plan: Building Brighter Futures. London: HMSO.
Douglas, J.W.B. (1964) *The Home and School*. London: MacGibbon.

Education Committee (2017) Recruitment and retention of teachers. February, HC199.

Elliott, B. and Calderhead, J. (1994) Mentoring for Teacher Development: Possibilities and Caveats. In McIntyre, D., Hagger, H. and Wilkin, M.P. (eds), *Mentoring: Perspectives on School Based Teacher Education*, 166–189. London: Kogan-Page.

Ellis, V.M., Maguire, M., Trippestad, T.M., Liu, Y., Yang, X. and Zeichner, K. (2015) Teaching Other People's Children, Elsewhere for a While: The Rhetoric of Travelling Educational Reform. *Journal of Education Policy*, Vol. 31, No. 1.

European Commission (2014) *Shaping Career-Long Perspectives on Teaching*. Brussels: European Commission.

Fletcher, S. (1995) Caveat Mentor. *Language Learning Journal*, Vol. 11, March.

Foster, R. (2001) The Graduate Teacher Route to QTS: Motorway, By-way or By-pass? Paper presented at the Annual Conference of the British Education Research Association, University of Leeds, 13–15 September.

Freedman, S., Lipson, B. and Hargreaves, D. (2008) *More Good Teachers*. London: Policy Exchange.

Fullan, M. (2012) What America Can Learn From Ontario's Education Success. *Atlantic*, 4 May. www.theatlantic.com/national/archive/2012/05/what-america-can-learn-from-ontarios-education-success/256654/.

Furlong, J. (2013) *Education: An Anatomy of the Discipline: Rescuing the University Project?* London: Routledge.

Furlong, J. and Oancea, A. (2005) *Assessing Quality in Applied and Practice-Based Educational Research: A Framework for Discussion*. Oxford: Oxford Department of Educational Studies.

Furlong, L., Barton, L., Miles, S., Whiting, C. and Whitty, G. (2000) *Teacher Education in Transition*. Philadelphia, PA: Oxford University Press.

Furlong, J., Campbell, A., Howson, J. and McNamara, O. (2006) Partnership in English Initial Teacher Education: Changing Times, Changing Definitions. Evidence from the Teacher Training Agency's National Partnership Project. *Scottish Educational Review*, Vol. 37, 32–45.

Furlong, J., Cochran-Smith, M. and Brennan, M. (eds) (2009) *Policy and Politics in Teacher Education: International Perspectives*. Abingdon: Routledge.

Galton, M., Simon, B. and Croll, P. (1980) *Inside the Primary Classroom*. London: Routledge and Kegan Paul.

Gambhir, M., Broad, K., Evans, M. and Gaskell, J. (2008) *Characterizing Initial Teacher Education in Canada: Themes and Issues*. Toronto: University of Toronto.

Gillard, D. (2011) Education in England: A Brief History. www.educationengland.org.uk/history (accessed January 2014).

Goldacre, B. (2013) *Building Evidence into Education*. London: DfE.

Gove, M. (2010) Speech to the National College Annual Conference, Birmingham, 16 June.

Gove, M. (2013) I Refuse to Surrender to the Marxist Teachers Hell-Bent on Destroying Our Schools. *Daily Mail*, 23 March. www.dailymail.co.uk/debate/article-2298146/.

Hall, D. (2013) Drawing a Veil over Managerialism: Leadership and the Discursive Disguise of the New Public Management. *Journal of Educational Administration and History*, Vol. 45, No. 3, 555–580.

Halsey, H.A. and Sylva, K. (1987) Plowden History and Prospects. *Oxford Education Review*, Vol. 13, No. 1, 3–11.

Hankey, J. (2004) The Good the Bad and Other Considerations: Reflections on Mentoring Trainee Teachers in Post Compulsory Education. *Research in Post Compulsory Education*, Vol. 9, No. 3, 389–400.

Hannan, A. (1995) The Case for School Led Primary Teacher Training. *Journal of Education for Teaching*, Vol. 21, No. 1, 25–35.
Hansard Deb 4 November 2015 c1634–1635.
Hargreaves, A. and Shirley, D. (2012) *The Global Fourth Way: The Quest for Educational Excellence*. London: SAGE.
Hargreaves, L. and Flutter, J. (2013) The Status of Teachers and the Teaching Profession: A Desk-Study for Education International. Unpublished manuscript, Department of Education, University of Cambridge.
HC Oral Evidence (2015) Supply of Teachers. Education Committee minutes, N. Gibb, 8 December.
Herrup, K. (2011) What We Can Learn from Canadians. http://blogs.reuters.com/great-debate/2011/08/24/what-we-can-learn-from-canadians/.
Higgins, S., Cordingley, P., Greany, T. and Coe, R. (2015) Developing Great Teaching: Lessons from the International Reviews into Effective Professional Development. Teacher Development Trust. http://tdtrust.org/about/dgt.
Ho, P. (2010) The Singapore Story. Presentation at the International Perspectives on US Education Policy and Practice Symposium, Washington, DC, 27–8 April.
HobsonA. and Malderez (2002) School Based Mentoring in Initial Teacher Training (ITT): What the Student Teachers Think. *NFER*, Vol. 28, 1–6.
Hobson, A. J., Ashby, P., Malderez, A. and Tomlinson, P.D. (2009) Mentoring Beginning Teachers: What We Know and What We Don't. *Teaching and Teacher Education*, Vol. 25, No. 1, 207–216.
Hogan, D. (2014) Why Is Singapore's School System so Successful, and Is It a Model for the West? *Conversation*. http://theconversation.com/why-is-singapores-school-system-so-successful-and-is-it-a-model-for-the-west-22917.
Hokka, P. and Etalapelto, A. (2013) Seeking New Perspectives on the Development of Teacher Education: A Study of the Finnish Context. *Journal of Teacher Education*, 17 September.
House of Lords Debate (1990) Vol. 517, cc 964–968, 29 March. London: HMSO.
Howson, J. (2015) Teacher Supply: Crisis, Challenge or No Problem? Oxford ITE Conference, 18 November.
Ingersoll, R. (ed.) (2007) A Comparative Study of Teacher Preparation and Qualifications in Six Nations. *CPRE*, February.
Junemann, C. and Ball, S.J. (2013) ARK and the Revolution of State Education in England. *Education Inquiry*, Vol. 4, No. 3, 423–441.
Kogan, M. (1987) The Plowden Report Twenty Years On. *Oxford Review of Education*, Vol. 13, No. 1.
KraftM. and PapayJ. (2014) Can Professional Environments in Schools Promote Teacher Development? Explaining Heterogeneity in Returns to Teaching Experience. *Educational Effectiveness and Policy Analysis*, Vol. 36, No. 4, 476–500.
Laukkenen, R. (2008) Finnish Strategy for High-Level Education for All. In Soguel, N.C. and Jaccard, P. (eds), *Governance and Performance of Education Systems*. London: Springer.
Lawlor, S. (1990) Teachers Mistaught: Training in Theories or Education in Subjects. *Centre for Policy Studies*, Vol. 116.
Lawson, J. and Silva, H. (1973) *A Social History of Education in England*. London: Methuen.
Le Grand, J. and Bartlett, W. (1993) *Quasi Markets and Social Policy*. Basingstoke: Macmillan.
Leaton-Gray, S. and Whitty, G. (2010) Social Trajectories or Disrupted Ideologies? Changing and Comparing Models of Teacher Professionalism under New Labour. *Cambridge Journal of Education*, Vol. 40, No. 1, 5–23.

Lee, J. and Fitz, J. (1997) HMI and Ofsted: Evolution or Revolution in School Inspection. *British Journal of Educational Studies*, Vol. 45, No. 1, 39–52.

Lowe, R. (1997) *Schooling and Social Change 1964–1990*. London: Routledge.

MacBeath, J. (2012) Teacher Training, Education or Learning by Doing in the UK. In Darling-Hammond, L. and Day, C. (eds), *Teacher Education around the World*. London: Routledge.

MacLeod, D. (1993) Teacher Training Standard Attacked. *Independent*, 22 January.

Maguire, M. (2014) Reforming Teacher Education in England: 'An Economy of Discourses of Truth'. *Journal of Education Policy*, Vol. 29, No. 6, 774–784.

Maguire, M. and George, R. (2017) Reforming Teacher Education in England: Locating the 'Policy' Problem. In Trippestad, T., Swennen, A. and Werler, T. (eds), *The Struggle for Teacher Education*. London: Bloomsbury.

Mahony, P. and Hextall, I. (2000) *Reconstructing Teaching*. London: Routledge Falmer.

Major, J. (1999) *The Autobiography*. London: Harper Collins.

Mawson, K. (2017) A Personal Reflection on Establishing a New Multi Author Blog and Its Role in Developing Research-Informed Teachers. *Warwick Journal of Education: Transforming Teaching*, Vol. 1, 103–109.

McKenzie, J. (2001) *Changing Education: A Sociology of Education since 1944*. Harlow: Pearson Education.

McKinsey & Co. (2007) *How the World's Best-Performing School Systems Come out on Top*. London: McKinsey.

McNamara, O., Murray, J. and Phillips, R. (2017) *Policy and Research Evidence in the 'Reform' of Primary Initial Teacher Education in England*. York: Cambridge Primary Review Trust.

McNicholl, J., Ellis, V. and Blake, A. (2013) Introduction to the Special Issue on the Work of Teacher Education: Policy, Practice and Institutional Conditions. *Journal of Education for Teaching, International Research and Pedagogy*, Vol. 39, No. 3, 260–265.

Menter, I. (2016) Introduction. In Beauchamp, G., Clarke, L., Hulme, M. et al. (eds), *Teacher Education Group: Teacher Education in Times of Change*. Bristol: Policy Press.

Menter, I., Hulme, M., Elliot, D. et al. (2010) *Literature Review on Teacher Education in the 21st Century*. Edinburgh: Scottish Government.

Middlewood, D. and Abbott, I. (2015) *Improving Profession Learning through In-House Inquiry*. London: Bloomsbury.

Middlewood, D. and Abbott, I. (2017) *Managing Staff for Improved Performance*. London: Bloomsbury.

Middlewood, D., Abbott, I. and Robinson, S. (2018) *Collaborative School Leadership*. London: Bloomsbury.

Minister for Employment and Learning (2014) Aspiring to Excellence: Final Report of the International Review Panel on the Structure of Initial Education in Northern Ireland. June.

Moore, A. (2004) *The Good teacher: Dominant Discourses in Teaching and Teacher Education*. London: Routledge Falmer.

Morris, E. (2013) Someone Needs to Inspect the Ofsted Inspectors. *Guardian*, 22 July.www.theguardian.com/education/2013/jul/22/school-inspections-ofsted-must-improve.

Morris, E. (2015) Determination Becomes Obstinacy at the Department of Education. *Guardian Education*, 23 November. www.theguardian.com.

Morris, P. (2012) Pick 'n' Mix, Select and Project: Policy Borrowing and the Quest for 'World Class' Schooling: An Analysis of the 2010 White Paper. *Journal of Education Policy*, Vol. 27, No. 1, 89–107.

Moyle, K. (2015) *Teacher Education in HPS*. Camberwell: Australian Council for Educational Research.

Murray, J. and Mutton, T. (2016) Teacher Education in England: Change in Abundance, Continuities in Question. In Beauchamp, G., Clarke, L., Hulme, M. et al. (eds), *Teacher Education Group: Teacher Education in Times of Change*. Bristol: Policy Press.

Musset, P. (2010) *Initial Teacher Education and Continuing Training Policies in a Comparative Perspective: Current Practices in OECD Countries and a Literature Review on Potential Effects*. Paris: OECD Publishing.

Mutton, T. (2016) Partnership in Teacher Education. In Beauchamp, G., Clarke, L., Hulme, M. et al. (eds), *Teacher Education Group: Teacher Education in Times of Change*. Bristol: Policy Press. Bristol: Policy Press.

Natale, C., Gaddis, L., Bassett, K. and McKnight, K. (2013) *Creating Sustainable Teacher Career Pathways: A 21st Century Imperative Overview*. London: Pearson and National Network of State Teachers of the Year.

National Association of Head Teachers (2018) School Funding in Crisis: Regional School Summits. Haywards Heath: NAHT.

National Audit Office (2016) Training New Teachers. HC798, February, 37.

NCEE (2016a) Empowered Educators – Canada: Diversity and Decentralisation. Washington, DC: NCEE.

NCEE (2016b) Empowered Educators – Finland: Constructing Teacher Quality. Washington, DC: NCEE.

NCEE (2016c) Empowered Educators – Shanghai: Culture, Policy and Practice. Washington, DC: NCEE.

NCEE (2016d) Empowering Educators: Recruiting and Selecting Excellent Teachers. Washington, DC: NCEE.

Nowotny, E. (1977) The Reorganisation of Teacher Education in the UK and Ontario: Implications for Australia. *Australian Journal of Teacher Education*, Vol. 2, No. 2.

Oates, T. (2015) Finnish Fairy Stories. *Cambridge Assessment*. www.cambridgeassessment.org.uk/images/207376-finnish-fairy-stories-tim-oates.pdf.

OECD (2010a) Shanghai and Hong Kong: Two Distinct Examples of Education Reform in China. www.oecd.org/countries/hongkongchina/46581016.pdf.

OECD (2010b) Strong Performers and Successful Reformers in Education: Lessons from PISA for the United States. www.oecd.org/pisa/46623978.pdf.

Ofsted (1993a) The Licenced Teacher Scheme Sept. 1990 to July 1992. London: HMSO.

Ofsted (1993b) The Articled Teacher Scheme Sept. 1990 to July 1992. London: HMSO.

Ofsted (2002) The Graduate Teacher Programme. London: HMSO.

Ofsted (2003) The Initial Training of Further Education Teachers: A Survey, HMI 17. London: HMSO.

Peiser, G. (2016) The Place of Research in Teacher Education. In Beauchamp, G., Clarke, L., Hulme, M. et al. (eds), *Teacher Education Group: Teacher Education in Times of Change*. Bristol: Policy Press.

Peters, R.S. (1959) *Authority, Responsibility and Education*. London: Allen and Unwin.

Phillips, D. and Schweisfurth, M. (2006) *Comparative and International Education: An Introduction to Theory, Method and Practice*. Trowbridge: Cromwell Press.

Pollard, A. (2014) REF 2014: What Does It Mean for Education and Educational Research. BERA.

Public Accounts Committee Report (2016) Training New Teachers. London: HMSO.

Ribbins, P. and Sherratt, B. (1997) *Radical Education Policies and Conservative Secretaries of State*. London: Cassell.

Rich, R.W. (1933) *The Training of Teachers in England and Wales during the Nineteenth Century*. London: Cambridge University Press.

Russell, B. (1946) *A History of Western Philosophy*. London: George Allen and Unwin.

Sahlberg, P. (2009) Educational Change in Finland. In Hargreaves, A., Fullan, M., Lieberman, A. and Hopkins, D. (eds), *International Handbook of Educational Change*. Dordrecht: Springer.

Sahlberg, P. (2010) Key Drivers of Educational Performance in Finland. Presentation at the International Perspectives on US Education Policy and Practice symposium, Washington, DC. http://asiasociety.org/education/learning-world/what-accounts-finland-high-student-achievement-rates.

Schleicher, A. (ed.) (2012) *Preparing Teachers and Developing School Leaders for the 21st Century: Lessons from around the World*. Paris: OECD Publishing.

Sharpe and Gopinathan (2002) After Effectiveness: New Directions in the Singapore School System? *Journal of Education Policy*, Vol. 17, No. 2, 151–166.

Sibieta, L. (2018) *The Teacher Labour Market in England: Shortages, Subject Expertise and Incentives*. London: Education Policy Institute.

Southern, A. (2018) Disrupting the habitus? Media Representations and Participant Experience of Teach First: An Exploratory Case Study in Wales. *Teachers and Training*, Vol 24, No. 5, 584–597.

Stewart, V. (2010/11) Raising Teacher Quality around the World. *Effective Educator*. Vol. 68, No. 4, 16–20.

Symeonidus, V. (2015) *The Status of Teachers and the Teaching Profession*. Brussels: Education International.

Tan, S.K.S., Wong, A.F.L., Gopinathan, S., Goh, K.C. and Wong, I.Y.F. (2007) The Qualifications of the Teaching Force: Data from Singapore. In Ingersoll, R. (ed.), *A Comparative Study of Teacher Preparation Qualifications in 6 Nations: China, Hong Kong, Japan, Korea, Singapore and Thailand*. CPRE.

Tan, T.H. (2015) *Is it Time for a New Approach to Education in Singapore? Towards Education for a Flourishing Life*. Singapore: HEAD Foundation.

Tatto, M.T. (2013) The Role of Research in International Policy and Practice in Teacher Education. *BERA*.

Tawney, R. (1914) *Secondary Education for All*. London: Bloomsbury.

Tawney, R. (1931) *Equality*. London: Harper Collins.

Taylor, W. (2008) The James Report Revisited. *Oxford Review of Education*, Vol. 34, No. 3, 291–311.

TDA (2006) *Improving Teacher Training Provision in England 1990–2006*. London: HMSO.

Trippestad, T.A., Swennen, A. and Werler, T. (eds) (2017) *The Struggle for Teacher Education: International Perspectives on Governance and Reforms*. London: Bloomsbury.

Tucker, M. (ed.) (2014a) *Chinese Lessons: Shanghai's Rise to the Top of the PISA League Tables*. Washington, DC: NCEE.

Tucker, M. (2014b) Shanghai: Teacher Quality Strategies. http://ncee.org/2014/02/tuckers-lens-lessons-in-teacher-quality-from-shanghai/.

Turner-Bissett, R.B. (2001) *Expert teaching*. London: David Fulton.

UCET (2013) *Westminster Education Forum: The Role of Universities in the New Initial Teacher Training Landscape*. London: UCET.

UNICEF Report Card 7 (2007) *Child Poverty in Perspective: An Overview of Child Well-Being in Rich Countries*. Florence: UNICEF Innocenti Research Centre.

Universities UK (2014) *The Impact of Initial Teacher Training Reforms on English Higher Education Institutions*. London: UUK.

Vernon, B. (1982) *Ellen Wilkinson*. London: Croom Helm.

Wheldall, K. (1974) Social Factors Affecting the Comprehension of Pre-School Children. Paper presented to the Education Section of the British Psychological Society, Edinburgh, September.

Whitby, K. (2010) *School Inspection: Recent Experiences in High Performing Education Systems*. Reading: CfBT Education Trust.

Whitty, G. (2014) Recent Developments in Teacher Education and Their Consequences for the 'University Project in Education'. *Oxford Review of Education*, Vol. 40, No. 4, 266–481.

Wigdortz, B. (2012) *Success against the Odds: Five Lessons in How to Achieve the Impossible: The Story of Teach First*. London: Short Books.

Wilkins, R. (2014) *Education in the Balance: Mapping the Global Dynamics of School Leadership*. London: Bloomsbury.

Winkley, D. (1975) From Condescension to Complexity. *Oxford Review of Education*, Vol. 13, No. 1, 45–54.

Woods, R.G. (1972) Philosophy of Education. In Woods, R.G. (ed.), *Education and Its Disciplines*. London: London University Press.

Zeichner, K. (2014) The Struggle for the Soul of Teaching and Teacher Education in the USA. *Journal of Education for Teaching*, Vol. 40, No. 5, 551–568.

Zhang, M., Ding, X. and Xu, J. (2016) *Developing Shanghai's Teachers*. Washington, DC: National Center on Education and the Economy.

INDEX

Note: Alphabetisation is word-by-word. 'St' is filed as Saint.

11-plus 20–21, 31

ability levels (pupils): class groupings 29; selective schools 20–21, 30–31
academic performance *see* education standards; student outcomes
academy schools 2; *see also* multi-academy trust
accreditation *see* qualifications
Advisory Committee for the Supply and Education of Teachers (ACSET) 47, 48
Advisory Committee for the Supply and Training of Teachers (ACSTT) 47
Advisory Council on the Training and Supply of Teachers 19, 22, 42
Alexander, Robin 61
all-graduate profession: historical context 22–24; James Report 42; master's-level qualifications 61; 'the Great Debate' 44
Anglican Church 14
apprenticeship model of training: China (Shanghai) 83; contemporary context 70; historical context 13–14, 15
area training authorities (ATAs) 16–17, 19, 41
Articled Teacher Scheme 50, 51–52, 53
autonomy *see* school autonomy; teacher autonomy

Bachelor of Education qualification: all-graduate profession 32; James Report 42; Robbins Report 27, 28; subject knowledge 36; 'the Great Debate' 44
Baker, Kenneth 50
Balls, Ed 61
Battersea Normal School 13
Bedfordshire University 114–116
Birmingham University 23, 27–28
Bishop Otter Teacher Training College 14
Black Papers 33, 43
Blair, Tony 46; *see also* Labour Party (1997-2010)
Blunkett, David 5, 59
Board of Education, historical context 15, 18
Brexit 66
Brighouse, Tim 48
Bristol University 19
budgets *see* spending on education

Callaghan, James 43, 46
Cambridge Primary Review 61–62
Cameron, David 65; *see also* Coalition government (2010-2015)
Canada (Ontario), comparative educational systems 77–79
Canley College Coventry 11, 17–18, 23, 28; *see also* Coventry College of Education
Canterbury Christ Church University 121
careers *see* continuous professional learning; promotion; recruitment
Carter Review 66–70

central advisory councils 18–19
centralisation: contemporary context 2; high-performing education systems 87; historical context 12, 14–16; teacher autonomy 5
Children and Their Primary Schools 26
Children's Plan 61
China (Shanghai), comparative educational systems 82–84
Church of England 14
Churchill, Winston 20
Circular 10/65 26, 30–31
Circular 4/98 53
Circular 7/73 42
Clegg, Alex 29
coaching, for leadership 126; *see also* mentoring
Coalition government (2010-2015) 61–62, 64–66
comparative educational systems: Canada (Ontario) 77–79; China (Shanghai) 82–84; Finland 80–82; international perspectives 76–77, 87–91; Singapore 84–86; South Korea 86–87
compensatory education programmes 34–35
'competent craftsperson' teachers 8
comprehensive system of secondary education 30–31, 33
consensus in education: curriculum 28–29; end of and its impacts 33–35; 'the Great Debate' 26, 43–45
Conservative government (1979-1997) 45, 46–55
Conservative government (2015-present) 65; *see also* Coalition government (2010-2015)
continuous professional learning: Canada (Ontario) 79; case study primary PGCE 93; China (Shanghai) 83; Finland 81; Higher Education based teacher training 135; high-performing education systems 88–89; Singapore 85; South Korea 86–87; Teach First 127, 130; teacher education focus 6–7
Council for National Academic Awards (CNAA) 28, 41, 42
Council for the Accreditation of Teacher Education (CATE) 48–50, 53
Coventry College of Education (previously Coventry Training College): historical context 19–20; James Report 42; practice in schools 38; Robbins Report 28; *see also* Warwick University Institute of Education
Crosland, Anthony 34

Crowther, Geoffrey, Sir 21
Crowther Report 21–22
curriculum: consensus in education 28–29; Council for the Accreditation of Teacher Education 50; education studies 23; historical context 11–12, 14; James Report 38–39; Plowden Report 31–32; political interference 3–5; primary schools 32, 61–62; subject knowledge 29–30; Teach First 127–128; teachers' role 89

deprived areas: positive discrimination 34–35; practice in schools 37–38; Teach First 120, 126, 129
Dewey, John 15–16
Diploma in Higher Education 42
Dyke Report 15

Eccles, David 20, 21, 22
economic growth, education for 12, 33, 43
Education Act (1899) 14–15
Education Act (1902) 15
Education Act (1918) 15
Education Act (1944) 15, 16–17, 18–19
education for all 11; *see also* equality/inequality in education
education for its own sake 12, 33
education priority areas (EPAs) 34–35
Education Reform Act (1988) 50
education standards: contemporary political context 65–66; political interference 3–4; teacher autonomy 5–6; 'the Great Debate' 43; *see also* student outcomes
education studies 23, 35–37
Educational Excellence Everywhere 72
educational technology 39
elementary school *see* primary schools
11-plus 20–21, 31
Elliot Foundation Academy Trust 115
Emergency Training Scheme 17–18, 19, 56
equality/inequality in education: education for all 11; positive discrimination 34–35; practice in schools 37–38; Robbins Report 26; Teach First 112, 120, 126, 129
European Union: Brexit 66; international perspectives 77
evidence-based teaching 67–68, 139
exit rates 71–72
experience *see* placements

feedback, China (Shanghai) 83
female teachers 14, 22
Finland: comparative educational systems 80–82; Higher Education based teacher

training 140–141; importance of inspection 137; schools running teacher education 7
four-year degree courses 27–28, 35, 44
A Framework for Expansion 42, 43
France, importance of inspection 137
Froebel, Friedrich 12
funding for training, main routes and options 70; *see also* spending on education

gatekeeper skills, Teach First 127
gender: case study primary PGCE 95–96; female teachers 14, 22; segregated training for men and women 19–20
Germany, importance of inspection 137
'good' teaching 7–9; *see also* high-quality teaching
Gove, Michael 66, 69, 75
government *see* centralisation; policy; spending on education
Graduate Teacher Scheme (GTS) 50, 55, 56–58
graduates as teachers: Bachelor of Education qualification 32; historical context 17, 21–22; James Report 42; Robbins Report 26–28; Teach First 59; 'the Great Debate' 44; *see also* all-graduate profession; Higher Education based teacher training
grammar schools 10, 20–21, 29, 33
'the Great Debate' 26, 43–45

Hadow, William, Sir 15–16
Hadow Reports 15
Hailsham, Viscount 20
Half Our Future 26, 29–30
Halsey, A. H. 34
Heath, Ted 33
higher educated teachers: education studies 35–36; historical context 21–22; Robbins Report 26–28; three- and four-year degree courses 27–28, 35, 44
Higher Education based teacher training: changing trends 2–3, 6; contemporary context 65, 68, 133–134, 135–136; Finland 80–81; future of 138–141, 142; high-performing education systems 89–90; historical context 13, 16–17; inspecting training 137, 138; James Report 41
Higher Education models of provision 92, 106–107; case study primary PGCE trainee 97–98; case study primary PGCE trainer 92–97; case study secondary PGCE trainee 104–106; case study secondary PGCE trainer 99–104
high-performing education systems (HPSs) 87–91; international perspectives 75, 76–77, 135; key practices 78
high-quality teaching 1; China (Shanghai) 82; contemporary political context 65; 'good' teaching 7–9; international perspectives 75; McNair Report 16
historical context 10–11, 24; 11-plus selection 20–21; 1962-1970 26–32; 1970-1979 33–45; central government involvement 12, 14–16; Coalition government (2010-2015) 61–62, 64–66; Conservative government (1979-1997) 45, 46–55; Crowther Report 21–22; education for all 11; expansion of educational spending 20; graduates as teachers 17, 22–24; Labour Party (1997-2010) 55–61; post-war years 18–20; teacher training in its infancy 11–13; training models and institutions 13–14; World War II 16–18
Home and Colonial School Society 13–14

Independent Report of the Primary Curriculum (IRPC) 61–62
induction: high-performing education systems 88–89; Warwick University PGCE case study 99–100
inequality *see* equality/inequality in education
infants *see* primary schools
in-service training, James Report 39, 40
inspecting training 54, 137; *see also* Office for Standards in Education, Children's Services and Skills (Ofsted)
institutions: Council for the Accreditation of Teacher Education 48–50; education studies 35–37; high-performing education systems 89–90; historical context 13–14; practice in schools 37–38; Robbins Report 26–28
international perspectives: Canada (Ontario) 77–79; China (Shanghai) 82–84; comparative educational systems 76–77, 87–91; Finland 80–82; Higher Education based teacher training 139–141; high-quality teaching 75; policy-borrowing process 75–76, 140; research focus 142; Singapore 84–86; South Korea 86–87
international rankings 76–77, 86, 90
Isaacs, Susan 15–16
Italy, importance of inspection 137

James Committee 25, 33, 44
James Report 25–26, 38–45
Joseph, Keith 46

Kelly, Ruth 56

Labour Party (1997-2010) 55–61
Lawlor, S. 36
leadership, Teach First 122, 125–126, 129
Leadership Development Programme 59, 121
learning support assistants 114
Leicester University PGCE case study 92–98
Lemov, Doug 127
libertarian values 33
Licenced Teacher Scheme 50–51, 53
living standards, historical context 21
local education authorities (LEAs): Circular 10/65 30–31; Graduate Teacher Scheme 55; historical context 15, 18, 19; James Report 41; neoliberalism 2; School-Centred Initial Teacher Training 54
London, Teach First 120, 123

Major, John 53–54
Maria Grey Teacher Training and Registration Society 14
market-led approach: neoliberalism 2, 3–5; performance-related pay 53–54; recruitment 47–48, 71–72; schools running teacher education 50–52; Teacher Development Agency 56; Teacher Training Agency 53–54
Mason, Charlotte 12–14
master's-level qualifications: expectation to have 61; Teach First 127, 130; Warwick University case study 101–104, *103*, 106; see also PGCE courses; post-graduate programmes
May, Theresa 66
McNair Report 16–17, 19, 26
mentoring: Articled Teacher Scheme 51–52; Carter Review 69–70; case study PGCEs 94, 105; models of training provision 113, 116–117; Teach First 130
Ministry of Education, historical context 18
models *see* Higher Education models of provision; school-based models of provision; Teach First; teacher training models
Modes of Teacher Education programmes 52–53
monitorial system, historical context 13, 15
Montessori, Maria 12, 15–16
Morgan, Nicky 75

Morris, Estelle 47–48
movement, Teach First 126
multi-academy trust (MAT) 2, 69

National Advisory Council on the Training and Supply of Teachers 19, 22, 42
National College for Teaching and Leadership (NCTL) 136
National Curriculum *see* curriculum
National School Society 13
Nene and Ramnoth School, Wisbech 114–119
neoliberalism 1–3; market-led approach 2, 3–5; school autonomy 2; teacher autonomy 5–6
the Netherlands, importance of inspection 137
New Public Management (NPM) 5
newly qualified teachers (NQTs): case study PGCEs 95, 104; models of training provision 109–110, 111
Newsom, John 29
Newsom Report 26, 29–30
Nuffield Foundation 38–39

Office for Standards in Education, Children's Services and Skills (Ofsted): case study primary PGCE 94; centralisation 2; contemporary context 137; Graduate Teacher Scheme 58; inspecting training 54–55; schools running teacher education 52–53; Teach First 123, 126–127
Ontario *see* Canada (Ontario)
Organisation for Economic Co-operation and Development (OECD) 77

parental involvement, education studies 37
partnerships, Carter Review 66–67
Patten, John 53
performance *see* education standards; student outcomes
performance-related pay 53–54
permissive society 25, 34
personal education, James Report 39–40
Pestalozzi, Johann Heinrich 12
PGCE courses: case study primary trainee 97–98; case study primary trainer 92–97; case study secondary trainee 104–106; case study secondary trainer 99–104; contemporary context 67; education studies 36; James Report 42; models of training provision 109–110, 111–113, 115; primary schools 31–32; Robbins Report 28

placements: Articled Teacher Scheme 50–52; case study PGCEs 94, 97–98, 104–105; historical context 37–38; Licenced Teacher Scheme 50–51, 53; models of training provision 115–117; research into 52–53; Teach First 122; *see also* schools running teacher education
Plowden Report 31–32, 34
Poland, importance of inspection 137
policy: Carter Review 66–70; China (Shanghai) 83–84; Conservative/Labour parties 46; contemporary political context 64–66, 73–74, 131–133; current training routes overview 70–73, 133–134; future of 141–142; high-performing education systems 87, 88; international perspectives 75–76, 140; market-led approach 3–5; recruitment 71–72; Singapore 85–86
policy-borrowing 75–76, 140
Pollard, Andrew 68
positive discrimination 34–35
post-graduate programmes: Finland 80; master's-level qualification expectations 61; South Korea 87; *see also* PGCE courses
post-graduate teaching apprenticeships 70
practice in schools *see* placements
pre-service training, James Report 39, 40
primary schools: Articled Teacher Scheme 51–52; Cambridge Primary Review 61–62; curriculum 32, 61–62; historical context 15–16; Independent Report of the Primary Curriculum 61–62; James Report 40–41; models of training provision 114–119; Plowden Report 31–32
professional development *see* continuous professional learning; teaching as a profession
Programme for International Student Assessment (PISA): Canada (Ontario) 78; international rankings 76; Singapore 84; South Korea 86
progressive methods 34, 36, 43
promotion: high-performing education systems 88; Singapore 85; Teach First 112, 127
provider-led training 70
public-sector reform 1–3; *see also* policy
purpose of education, historical context 12

qualifications: China (Shanghai) 82–83; Council for the Accreditation of Teacher Education 48–50; Crowther Report 21–22; expectation to have master's-level 61; Finland 80; Graduate Teacher Scheme 58; Half Our Future 29–30; historical context 17; primary schools 31–32; Robbins Report 26–28; Singapore 84–85; South Korea 86; subject knowledge 36; 'the Great Debate' 44; towards an all-graduate profession 22–24
qualified teacher status (QTS): contemporary context 67; Finland 80; inspecting training 137; models of training provision 115; Teach First 122
quality *see* high-quality teaching

recruitment: Canada (Ontario) 79; Conservative government (1979-1997) 47–48; Finland 81; high-performing education systems 88–89; historical context 17, 22; James Report 39; Licenced Teacher Scheme 51, 53; main routes and options 70–73; market-led approach 47–48, 71–72; models of training provision 111, 112, 118–119; policy 71–72; Singapore 85; Teach First 111–112, 122; *see also* teacher numbers
'reflective practitioner' teachers 8
Reform Act 1833 12
research into teacher training 52–53, 67–69
Robbins Report: commissioning 24, 25; implications 26–29
Russell, Bertrand 11

St Mary's College Cheltenham: all-graduate profession 23–24; Bristol University 19; founding 11, 14; as part of Gloucester University 56–57; post-war years 18; practice in schools 37; Robbins Report 28; Training College Association 15
salaries for teachers: deprived areas 35; historical context 22; performance-related 53–54; School Direct route 118
'saviour teachers' 8
school autonomy 2
School Direct 114–119, 133, 135–136, 142
school direct training 70
school leaving age 15, 18, 33
school-based models of provision 108, 119; primary 114–119; secondary 109–114
school-based teacher educators 134–135
School-Centred Initial Teacher Training (SCITT) programme 54, 55
Schools Council 38–39
schools running teacher education 2–3; Carter Review 69–70; case study PGCEs 93–94, 99, 104–105; contemporary

context 65, 72–73, 132, 133–134; Finland 80–81; future of 140, 142; Graduate Teacher Scheme (GTS) 57–58; historical context 13; inspecting training 137, 138; James Report 41; market-led approach 4–5; political bias 50–52; research into 52–53; teaching as a technical activity or profession 7
school-to-school networks 79
secondary schools: comprehensive system 30–31, 33; grammar schools 10, 20–21, 29, 33; James Report 41; models of training provision 109–114
selection processes: Finland 81; high-performing education systems 88–89; Teach First 122; *see also* recruitment
selective schools: 11-plus 20–21, 31; 1970s debates 33; comprehensive system of secondary education 30–31; Half Our Future 29; McNair Report 16
Shanghai *see* China (Shanghai)
Shephard, Gillian 53, 54
Singapore: comparative educational systems 84–86; Higher Education based teacher training 140, 141
sixth form colleges 30–31
Slovenia, importance of inspection 137
social status *see* status of teachers
South Korea: comparative educational systems 86–87; Higher Education based teacher training 140, 141
specialist subjects, primary 93
spending on education: Canada (Ontario) 78; Circular 10/65 32; historical context 15, 20; James Report 41; Teach First 59; 'the Great Debate' 44; *see also* funding for training
Spens Report 15
standards *see* education standards; qualifications
status of teachers: China (Shanghai) 82; high-performing education systems 88; South Korea 86
Student Associates Scheme 56
student outcomes: Finland 81; 'good' teaching 8; international rankings 76–77, 86, 90; Singapore 84; Teach First 123, 125; *see also* education standards
subject knowledge: contemporary context 65, 67, 72–73; Half Our Future 29–30; historical context 32; National Curriculum 53; PGCE course 36; practice in schools 52–53; qualifications 36; *see also* curriculum

summer institute (SI), Teach First 122, 124–125, 129

Teach First: history of 59, 120–121; impact 122–124; mission and criticism 120; as model 121–122; new model 126–128; participant perspective 129–130; programme 124–126; school case study 110, 111–113; theory and practice 2
teacher autonomy: historical context 18; neoliberalism 5–6; Schools Council 39
Teacher Development Agency (TDA): Labour Party (1997-2010) 60–61; market-led approach 56–57; schools running teacher education 50; success of 62; Teach First 59
teacher education focus 6–7; contemporary context 65, 67–69; historical context 11–13; leadership 122, 125–126, 129; *see also* subject knowledge
Teacher Education Model, Singapore 84
teacher numbers: Canada (Ontario) 79; case study primary PGCE 92–93; Circular 10/65 30–31; Conservative government (1979-1997) 47–48; contemporary context 71–72; Crowther Report 21–22; Finland 81; James Report 42; Labour Party (1997-2010) 58–59; main routes and options 70–73; Robbins Report 26, 27–29; towards an all-graduate profession 23–24; Warwick University PGCE case study 99, **100**; *see also* recruitment
teacher research group, China 83
teacher status *see* status of teachers
Teacher Training Agency (TTA): contemporary context 136; Labour Party (1997-2010) 60; market-led approach 53–54; schools running teacher education 50; success of 62; teacher numbers 58–59
teacher training models: historical context 13–14; Leicester University PGCE case study 92–98; overview of routes and options 70–73, 133–134; Warwick University PGCE case study 99–106; *see also* Higher Education models of provision; school-based models of provision
teaching as a profession 7; historical context 13, 14; towards an all-graduate profession 22–24; *see also* promotion; qualifications
teaching as a technical activity 7
teaching assistants 114
teaching methods, James Report 38–39
technician side of teaching *see* teaching as a technical activity

technology, educational 39
Thatcher, Margaret 23, 33, 47; *see also* Conservative government (1979-1997)
Three Wise Men report 34, 61
three-year degree courses 27–28, 35, 44
training *see headings under* teacher training
Training College Association 15, 23
Trends in International Mathematics and Science Study (TIMSS) 76–77

UNICEF 61
United Kingdom: importance of Ofsted 137, 138; market-led approach 3–5; neoliberalism 1–3; teacher autonomy 5–6; teacher education focus 6; teaching as a technical activity or profession 7
universities *see* graduates as teachers; Higher Education based teacher training

unqualified teachers, models of training provision 109–110, 111–112, 114
urban schools, practice in 37–38

Warwick University Institute of Education 37, 56, 68
Warwick University PGCE case study 99–106
Wilkinson, Ellen 17, 18
Williams, Shirley 43, 46
Wilson, Harold 33
Wisbech Schools Partnership 115
women teachers 14, 22
Woodhead, Chris 54–56
Woods, R. G. 35–36
Worcester College/University: Emergency Training Scheme 18, 56; founding 11; Robbins Report 27–28; specialist subjects 23
World War II 16–18

Printed in Great Britain
by Amazon